Shiva to Shankara

Decoding the Phallic Symbol

D1607787

Shiva to Shankara

Decoding the Phallic Symbol

Dr. Devdutt Pattanaik

Indus Source Books

Indus Source Books
PO Box 6194
Malabar Hill PO
Mumbai 400 006
INDIA
Email: info@indussource.com
www.indussource.com

ISBN 10: 81-88569-04-6
ISBN 13: 978-81-88569-04-5

First edition August 2006
First reprint June 2009
Second reprint October 2010

All rights reserved
Printed at Decora Book Prints Pvt. Ltd., Mumbai

CONTENTS

Note from the author   *vi*

INTRODUCTION
Phallic but not fertile   1

ISOLATION OF SHIVA
The hermit withdraws from the world in the quest for serenity
and stillness   5

SEDUCTION OF SHIVA
The hermit finally marries the Goddess and engages with the
world   53

GRACE OF SHIVA
The hermit becomes the accessible and benevolent householder
called Shankara   103

CONCLUSION
Deconstructing destruction   154

Bibliography   156

NOTE FROM THE AUTHOR

Hinduism is not a static religion. It has evolved with history.

In its earlier form, it was known as the Vedic religion, a religion of a pastoral people, commonly identified as the Aryans. Their primary religious activity involved invoking a primal abstract force known as Brahman through a ritual known as yagna, to satisfy various material aspirations. Hymns were chanted and offerings made into a fire-altar in the quest for fertility and power. That the ritual involved no permanent shrine suggests its followers were a nomadic people.

Hinduism today is very rooted to the land. It revolves around a shrine, often a vast temple complex. This shift is ascribed to the mingling of the Aryans, over 2000 years ago with agriculturists, city dwellers, and forest tribes, a process which continued over a thousand years. Tantalising glimpses of the assimilation process emerge from chronicles and epics written only in the last millennia.

The most spectacular shift in the nature of Hinduism has been the move from almost agnostic ritualism to unabashed theism: from belief in a host of gods and spirits to belief in an all-powerful God.

But like all things Indian, this belief was not so simple. Hindus visualised the all-powerful God in various ways. For some, God was the world-affirming Vishnu. For others, God was the world-rejecting Shiva. And then there were those for whom God was feminine, the Goddess. The Gods co-existed with the Goddess and the gods and the spirits. Nothing was rejected. This was the Hindu way.

The first evidence of Shiva comes from the pre-Vedic era, from a seal from the Indus Valley civilisation. It shows a naked man with an erect penis, sitting in the yogic "throne" position or Bhadrasana, wearing horned headgear, surrounded by animals. Since the script has not been deciphered one can only speculate what this image represents. But most scholars believe it is an early form of Shiva because it captures at least three attributes of Shiva: Shiva as Pashupati, lord of animals; as Yogeshwara, lord of yoga; and as Lingeshwara, lord of the phallus.

In early Vedic scriptures, conservatively dated 1500 BC, Shiva is known as Rudra. He is a god who is feared. He howls and shoots arrows that spread disease. He is appeased and requested to stay away. In the Shatarudriya hymn of the Yajur Veda there is a sense that he is considered highly potent and highly dangerous. In the Brahmanas one is told "His name shall not be spoken". He remains an outsider god—a god to whom the leftovers of the yagna have to be offered. This, and the existence of pre-Vedic representations of Shiva, have led to speculation that Shiva is perhaps not a Vedic god. Perhaps he was a tribal god or perhaps a god of settled agricultural communities, the Dravidians, who were overrun by Aryans. The reluctant, and perhaps violent, entry of Shiva into the Vedic pantheon is believed to have given rise to the tale of the desecration of Daksha's yagna by Shiva. It represents the uneasy relationship between exoteric Vedic rituals on one hand and esoteric Dravidian practices such as yoga, asceticism and alchemy.

In the 5th century BC, Buddhism and Jainism posed a great threat to Vedic ritualism. Members of the merchant classes patronized these monastic ideologies. Threatening even the Buddhists and the Jains was the idea of an all powerful personal Godhead that was slowly taking shape in the popular imagination. The common man always found more comfort in tangible stories and rituals that made trees, rivers, mountains, heroes, sages, alchemists and ascetics worthy of worship. The move from many guardian deities and fertility spirits to one all-powerful uniting deity was but a small step.

Being atheistic, or at least agnostic, Buddhism and Jainism could do nothing more than tolerate this fascination for theism on their fringes. In a desperate bid to survive, Vedic priests, the Brahmins, did something more: they consciously assimilated the trend into the Vedic fold. In their speculation they concluded and advertised the idea that Godhead was nothing but the embodiment of Brahman, the mystic force invoked by the chanting of Vedic hymns and the performance of Vedic rituals. Adoration of this Godhead through pooja, a rite that involved offering food, water, flowers, lamp, and incense, was no different from the yagna. Vedanta metaphysics was allegorised so that param-atma was not just an abstract concept; it was personified in Godhead. In the Shvetavastra Upanishad, Shiva is without doubt Brahman, the cosmic consciousness. With this association, Vedism transformed into what is now known as classical Hinduism. It was a transformation that ensured that Vedic ideology survived the Buddhist and Jain onslaught.

The Vedic gods, such as Indra and Agni, were sidelined. All attention was given to Shiva and Vishnu, forms of Godhead, whose story was told and retold and finally compiled in Sanskrit chronicles known as the Puranas.

The middle ages saw great rivalry between Shiva-worshippers and Vishnu-worshippers. In the Shiva Purana and Linga Purana, Shiva is often shown as the real force behind the power of Vishnu. The theme is reversed in the Vishnu Purana and the Matysa Purana. So great was the rivalry that Vishnu-worshippers wore vertical caste marks while Shiva-worshippers wore horizontal caste marks; Vishnu-worshippers painted their house with vertical strokes while Shiva-worshippers painted their houses with horizontal strokes; Vishnu-worshippers kept the Tulsi in their house while Shiva-worshippers kept the Bilva plant. People who worshipped Vishnu refused to marry or dine with those who worshipped Shiva.

There were, of course, many attempts at reconciliation such as the cult of Hari-Hara, the simultaneous worship of Vishnu and Shiva, that become popular around the 15th century. Even the 16th century classic, Tulsi Ramayana, makes an overt attempt to show that Shiva and Vishnu are one and the same Godhead that cares for humanity.

Today, the rivalry between Shiva-worshippers and Vishnu-worshippers is not very evident except perhaps in the temple complexes of Tamil Nadu and in the traditions of the Iyers and the Ayyangars. Though both Shiva and Vishnu are considered forms of Godhead, no Hindu will ever interchange Shiva for Vishnu.

Stories, symbols, and rituals, especially the ones deemed sacred, construct for a people a way of making sense of the world. The concept of Shiva constructed by sacred stories, symbols, and rituals is quite different from the idea of Vishnu. Shiva is always a reluctant groom whom the Goddess has to force into marriage. His children are not produced "normally". Vishnu, on the other hand, is surrounded by women. As Rama, he protects them. As Krishna, he flirts with them. While Shiva is associated with snow-capped mountains and caves and crematoriums, Vishnu is associated with meadows and rivers and battlefields. Whereas Shiva surrounds himself with dogs, bulls, ashes, skulls, animal skins, and narcotics, Vishnu is found amid cows, horses, silks, flowers, pearls, gold and sandal paste. Shiva does not want to be part of society; Vishnu, on the other hand, establishes the code of conduct for society. In temples, Vishnu is visualized as a king. His anthropomorphic image is bedecked with gold and devotees can see him only from afar. Shiva, on the other hand, is enshrined in open temples. Devotees are free to walk in and pour water on the oval stone or cylinder that represents him. Vishnu is offered butter and sweets, Shiva is given only raw milk. Clearly, Shiva is associated with ascetic ideals while Vishnu is associated with worldly thoughts.

Disdain for the material world is a dominant theme in philosophical schools that consider Shiva as their patron deity. This disdain manifests in two ways: asceticism and alchemy. The former seeks to outgrow all things material and reunite with Shiva. The latter seeks to control the material world and make it do its bidding. Kashmir Shaivism of Nepal, Shiva Siddhanta of Tamil Nadu, and the Lingayat and Vira-Shaiva movements of Karnataka tilt towards ascetic ideologies while Tantrik sects such as the Pashupatas, Kapalikas and Kanphatas tilt towards alchemical principles. In the former, sexual activity is shunned; in the latter sexual activity is merely an occult ritual. Neither gives much thought to the pleasurable and procreative aspects of sex.

And yet, Shiva is represented by a very sexual symbol: the male reproductive organ placed within the female reproductive organ. Why? The quest for the answer has made me write this book.

Of course, the easy route is to accept the most common and simplistic explanation: it is a fertility symbol. But to make sense of a mythological image one has to align the language heard (stories) with the language performed (rituals) and the language seen (symbols). All dissonances have to be removed so that the real meaning can be deciphered.

Any attempt to seek "true" meaning behind the sexual imagery may be seen as an exercise in prudishness. Hindus have long been embarrassed by Shiva's phallic representation. For centuries it has been used to make people defensive and apologetic. Society has always been uncomfortable with sex, terrified by its primal nature. This book can be seen as yet another effort to shy away from the obvious. Maybe it is. Or maybe it is a chance to discover a deeper meaning in a manner not explored before.

Dr. Devdutt Pattanaik

INTRODUCTION: PHALLIC BUT NOT FERTILE

In the Veda, Shiva is described as Maha-deva, the great god who is none other than God.

In Tantra, Shiva needs Shakti, the Goddess, to enliven his divinity. He lies as dormant as a corpse until she sits on him, arouses him, and forces him to copulate. The copulation is so intense that Shiva does not pause even when sages pay him a visit. Unable to realise the significance of this continual—and rather immodest—union, the sages decide to meditate on Shiva, visualizing him as a linga.

A linga is a natural rock projection pointing skywards, a smooth oval stone collected from a riverbed, or a well-carved cylindrical shaft, placed in a leaf-shaped basin. When a devotee enters the shrine and faces the linga, he finds the snout of the basin always pointing to the left of the linga, draining water that drips continuously on the shaft from a perforated pot hanging from the ceiling.

The story goes that the primal artisan, Vishwakarma, stood before a cylindrical shaft, intent on carving the perfect form of God. But he realised that the magnificence of divinity could not be contained in an icon, so he placed the shaft in a basin and declared this aniconic representation as the "linga"—which literally means "attribute"—of that which has no attribute.

This narrative strips the Shiva-linga of all sexual significance. Millions of devotees who pour water on the linga with great affection and veneration fail to associate the linga with anything erotic. Yet, most scholars and scriptures, whether Vedic or Tantrik, identify the linga as a representation of Shiva's manhood. The basin, they say, represents the yoni or womb of the Goddess. Hindu women seeking a husband or children are advised to worship Shiva in this form. It is therefore easy to equate Shiva with the Egyptian Min or the Roman Priapus whose erect penis was venerated—so anthropologists and historians claim—as "a source of life and libido, as creator and miracle worker". Such a comparison, though convenient, is inconsistent with ideas expressed in the imagery, narratives, and philosophy of Shiva.

If Shiva were simply a fertility god, would his abode not be a sylvan retreat rather than a snow-clad mountain? Would he not be associated with romance and delight rather than meditation and austerity? Would he not be called "creator" rather than "destroyer"? Would he not be represented by life-sustaining water rather than life-claiming fire? Clearly, there is more to Shiva than meets the eye.

Shiva has to be seen in the light of both Vedic and Tantrik schools of Hinduism. The former is inward-looking and monastic. The latter is outward looking and more worldly. The former looks at the material world as delusion. The latter looks at the material world as the source of all power and wisdom. In the Veda, the Goddess is Maya, a temptation. In the latter, the Goddess is Shakti, power personified, the medium of the divine. How does Shiva respond to the Goddess? Why does he shut his eye to her charms? Why does she seek to arouse him?

Eroticism flavours Shiva's narratives, symbols and rituals. This grabs the attention, rouses the senses, primes the mind, and after the initial titillation—and outrage—has passed, allows for the effortless understanding of complex and perplexing metaphysical ideas encoded within this rich, mythical vocabulary. What blossoms eventually is an enchanting understanding of life, free from the angst of existence, filled only with peace—with the world, with oneself, and with divinity.

This book traces the journey of God from Shiva to Shankara, from being a hermit to being a householder. It seeks to decode the mystery of the divine "erotic ascetic" and his sacred symbol, the linga, by exploring narratives, symbols, and rituals associated with him.

Within infinite myths lies the
Eternal Truth
But who sees it all?
Varuna has but a thousand eyes
Indra has a hundred
And I, only two

ISOLATION OF SHIVA

*The hermit withdraws from the world in the quest for
serenity and stillness*

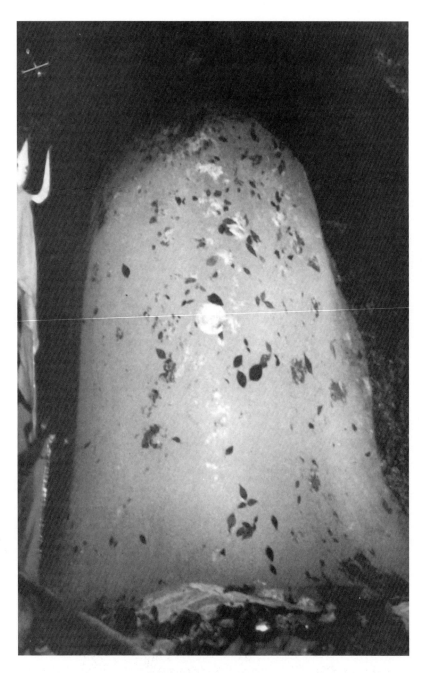

The ice Shiva-linga at Amarnath cave.

1

ISOLATION OF SHIVA

There is a force in the cosmos—one that has neither name nor form yet nourishes all that has a name or a form. It is neither contained by space nor bound by time. Yet, it makes space three-dimensional and time sequential. Ancient Indian seers, known as rishis, called this power Brahman. They accessed this power through the Veda, a body of self-created, self-communicating, mystical hymns.

Four thousand years ago, priests known as Brahmins incorporated these hymns in a ceremony known as the yagna. Offerings were made into fire so that the smoke carried the power of Brahman to a race of celestial beings known as devas, who dwelt in the skies. Energized by this ritual, the devas drew out life-giving sap or rasa in the form of water, minerals, and plants from beneath the surface of the earth.

For the Brahmins, devas were "gods" because their action nourished and sustained living organisms or jiva. Their pantheon was populated by the sun-god Surya, the moon-god Chandra, the wind-god Vayu, the fire-god Agni and the king of devas, the thunderbolt-hurling rain-god Indra. There were hymns and offerings for each one of them during the yagna. But there were none for asuras, subterranean beings who were deemed "demons" because they withheld rasa under the earth's surface in the form of inorganic elements, the ajiva.

Then there was Shiva, sitting in absolute isolation on top of a snow-capped mountain at the centre of the universe, unmindful of the cycle

Through the ritual known as yagna, the Brahmins made offerings through fire to the devas. *Image Courtesy: R. G. Singh, Mysore.*

of rasa around him. His eyes were shut, his body still, his hair matted, his limbs smeared with ash. Shiva defied categorisation. Unmoved by the blooming and withering of life, the drawing and withdrawing of rasa, he seemed neither god nor demon. He appeared passive, inert, cold, and lifeless, like the icy mountain he sat on. Who could love or hate a being such as Shiva who seemed to live a purposeless existence, who possessed no standards, and hence valued nothing?

Bhikshatana: Shiva as the beggar-god who wanders the world with dogs and ghosts. *Temple carving, Tanjore.*

Shiva is not part of this world. He does not want to be part of the world. He is indifferent to its niceties. He has transcended human values and hierarchies. For members of society, he appears a beggar. But beggars want alms. Shiva wants nothing. *Illustration by author.*

DAKSHA INSULTED
[SHIVA PURANA]

Daksha, the patriarch of Vedic culture, commanded the respect of all. One day, he was invited to a gathering of gods. As Daksha entered, proud and noble, all the gods rose. They joined their hands to salute this supreme patron of the yagna. Daksha was pleased. He swept a glance around the assembly, accepting the salutations of the gods. Then his glance fell upon a solitary, seated figure and his expression darkened. He looked upon Shiva who continued to remain seated. Shiva did not want to insult Daksha, but he remained seated because he was oblivious to Daksha's exalted position. He was not impressed by the arrival of the patriarch, nor was he disdainful. He was simply indifferent, untouched by it all.

Daksha, however, was not amused. He expected the same reverence from Shiva that he received from the other gods. At that moment, he swore never to invite Shiva to any yagna. He deemed Shiva to be the outsider, unfit for prayer, praise, or sacrifice.

Metal masks are used in parts of Maharashtra and Karnataka to cover the Shiva linga. Typically, they sport moustaches and represent virile warriors. These masks indicate that the formless deity (linga) has eyes and can see the suffering of the devotee.

For all his indifference to the world, Shiva's manhood stood firm and erect. This conventionally suggested arousal by external stimuli, and it confounded many.

Seals found in the Indus Valley show images of men sitting in yogic postures among animals, sporting an erect phallus. This could suggest that the idea of the self-contained Shiva at bliss with himself was prevalent almost 4000 years ago when the Indus valley cities flourished. That the man has a trident-like headgear further indicates it could be proto-Shiva. Scholars sometimes identify this image as Pashupati, the lord of the beasts. There are anthropologists who believe that Shiva was originally not a Vedic god but forced his way into the Vedic pantheon.

CASTRATION OF SHIVA
[LINGA PURANA]

One day, Shiva came out of meditation and wandered into the forest. As he walked along, he chanced upon a hermitage. This hermitage, tucked away in a quiet nook of the forest, was home to a sage.

When Shiva came to the hermitage he found that there was a yagna in progress. Many sages had assembled there along with their wives. The flames of the sacrificial fire leapt high amid the chanting of sacred mantras. Shiva stepped forward and his presence was noticed at once— Shiva was naked and his penis was erect. The assembly gaped in astonishment. As the sages looked on in consternation, unsure of what to do, their wives decided to abandon all modesty. They were so smitten by Shiva's beauty and powerful presence that they ran after him and sought his embrace.

Slowly coming out of their stupefaction, the infuriated sages rushed at Shiva. They attacked him, wanting to castrate him for the wanton behaviour of their wives. Suddenly, Shiva's manhood transformed into a pillar of fire that threatened to set ablaze the hermitage and the world with it.

The sages and their wives were so distracted by Shiva's erect penis that they did not pay attention to the man behind it. They failed to see that Shiva's body lacked the tension of a man who seeks to embrace, penetrate, and spill semen.

Hindu artists have long used the penis or linga to represent the mental state, while storytellers have used the flow of semen as a metaphor for the mental process. Erection represents a mind drawn to things material;

Early North Indian images of Shiva dated 9th century AD depict him not only with an erect phallus but also bearing a staff. Both reflect the axis of the world, the soul, from which life emanates and around which the world revolves. These images are known as Lakulesha, the staff bearer, sometimes identified with Shiva and sometimes with Lakulesha, an early teacher of Shaiva lore.

flaccidity represents the reverse. Spilling of seed indicates submission to sensory stimuli; its retention indicates the reverse. Shiva's phallus is aroused but his eyes are shut. According to scriptures, his semen moves in the reverse direction, a condition known as urdhva-retas. Thus, in Shiva, the mind is stirred, but not by external stimuli.

Shiva's linga is svayambhu, self-stirred, spontaneous, resulting from the realisation of sat, the true nature of all things. This realisation happens when chitta or consciousness has been purged of ego, memories, desires, and all sources of conditioning that delude the mind. What follows is ananda, tranquility unconditioned by external influences. Shiva's spontaneous and autonomous erection, unaccompanied by any sign of excitement in the rest of his body, is an artistic expression of the state of sat-chitta-ananda, the state when one is in touch with Brahman. Immersed in the state of sat-chitta-ananda, Shiva is self-contained; he feels no urge to react to worldly enchantments or shed his semen.

Semen, according to Tantra, is nothing but a form of rasa. Rasa in minerals is transformed into sap by plants. Devas facilitate this process while asuras oppose it. Hence, they battle constantly. In the bodies of animals and humans, the sap of plants is transformed serially into plasma, blood, flesh, bone, nerve, and finally seed. The seed of woman is known as egg while the seed of man is known as semen. Unshed seed, transformed into ojas or energy in the human body, is spent as the jiva interacts with the environment. Thus, rasa which enters living creatures in the form of food—be it the nutrients of the soil, the sap of plants, or the flesh of animals—returns to the environment as energy spent during any worldly interaction. This cyclical flow of rasa sustains the wheel of life.

Rasa, that enters the body through food, re-enters the world when it is shed to produce new life. Women shed the egg involuntarily at the time of ovulation, like plants at the time of pollination and animals when they are in heat. But men control the flow of seed by will. The human male can be a bhogi, submit to desire and shed his seed following sensory stimulation, or he can be a yogi, triumph over desire and retain his seed. This unique physiology of the human male (contradicted by modern science though) made him, in the eyes of Hindu seers, the perfect symbol of the "individual" in Hindu mythology. Just as the human male can control the flow of semen, every individual —man or woman—can choose his/her responses to the world around. Acceptance of this metaphor transforms the impassive ithyphallic Shiva into that individual who has overcome all worldly stimuli, represented by the reverse semen flow, and has attained that much-desired goal of self-realisation and self-containment or sat-chitta-ananda, the self-stirred phallus.

Shiva neither sheds seed nor spends energy. Energy simply accumulates in his body as heat, as he stays away from all worldly interactions until

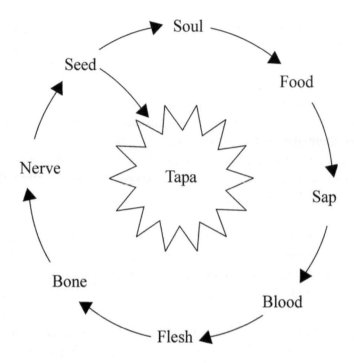

According to the Upanishads, the whole world is food, feeding on each other. This flow of matter and energy from inorganic to organic and back to inorganic form is the cycle of rasa. One can be part of this cycle by depending on it for sustenance and by contributing to its sustenace. Or like Shiva, withdraw from it totally. Not eating. Not breathing. Not spilling semen. This withdrawal is expressed as the reverse flow of semen that lights the spiritual fire of tapa.

it sets alight the spiritual fire known as tapa. The practice of churning tapa is known as tapasya and the fire-churner is known as tapasvin. Tapa throws light on the true nature of reality, burns all that deludes the consciousness, and stills the mind with tranquility. Tapasya thus leads to the triple goal of sat-chitta-ananda.

When the sages tried to castrate Shiva, the greatest of all tapasvins, the linga revealed its true form—not a tool of material pleasure but the churn of spiritual fire.

Every jiva inhabits samsara, the world experienced through the five senses. This world seems like a miserable and unhappy place; everything is uncertain and temporary. To allay suffering, a jiva performs actions, acts of self-preservation, self-propagation, and self-actualisation that offer life the promise of certainty, hope, and meaning. Each action is, in metaphorical terms, "shedding of semen", and involves expenditure of rasa. The jiva hopes that interaction with samsara will ultimately bring shanti, peace, a coming to terms with the apparent meaninglessness of existence. Shanti is the layman's word for the rather metaphysical phrase: sat-chitta-ananda.

But when semen is shed, a child is born. For every response to stimuli, there is a reaction, one that the jiva is obliged to experience either in this lifetime or the next. So states the universal law of karma. The jiva is thus dragged through lifetimes of experiences until the karmic debt is repaid. The cycle of rebirth rotates ceaselessly as the jiva keeps responding to the tantalizing provocations of samsara in the perpetual quest for shanti.

The fire of tapa, churned by the tapasvin, seeks to give the jiva the power to pause between stimulus and response. Rather than spilling the seed because of conditioned reflexes, the mind ponders on the stimuli and chooses the response that will bring shanti. Tapa thus trains the mind to yoke instinct with intellect. The act of yoking the mind is known as yoga. Yoga is tapasya. It lights the fire of tapa. In the light of tapa, the jiva realises that an event is a reaction to past events. It is identified and valued depending on one's experiences and expectations. If the experience and expectation is different, the same event comes to have a different identity and value. With the gradual incineration of delusions, the chitta is purified, sat is realised, and ananda is experienced. The jiva feels no urge to contribute to the cycle of reactions and rebirths. As a result, no more karma is generated. There is nothing that binds the jiva to the external world. With this comes shanti and ultimately moksha, liberation from the cycle of rebirths.

According to Tantra, the body or sharira that is reborn has three components:

- The sthula sharira or physical sheath, made up of five sense organs (eye, ear, tongue, nose, and skin) and five action organs (hands, legs, mouth, anus, and genitals)
- The sukshma sharira or mental sheath, made up of the mind, which houses the intellect, the ego, learning, memories, and desires
- The karana sharira or causal sheath, which retains all memories of actions performed by the jiva.

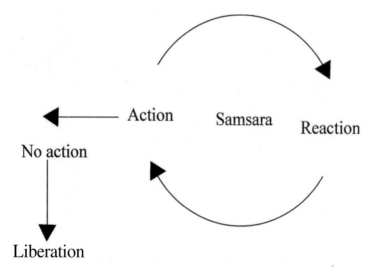

The material world is governed by the law of karma according to which nothing in the world happens spontaneously. All events are reactions to actions done in the past. Every action has a reaction that one is obliged to experience, if not in this life then in the next. One has the choice: to either react to an event or be indifferent to it. The householder reacts; the hermit stays indifferent.

When a person dies, what perishes is his physical body that can be seen and the mental body which animates the physical body. What does not die is the causal body, the seat of memories that propels the soul into the next life. The practice of tapasya aims to destroy the third body too, an idea that is expressed allegorically in the following narrative.

Shiva's indifference to all things worldly results in entropy. With no action, there is no reaction. With no reaction, rasa stops flowing. The world ceases to be. Shiva is called the great archer, whose bow Pinaka, is the symbol of yoga, his focussed, steadfast, inward attention. Using this bow, Shiva destroys all the three worlds that man inhabits as well as the three bodies that man possesses. *Illustration by author.*

SHIVA DESTROYS THE THREE CITIES
[SHIVA PURANA]

Once, three asuras, in their attempt at invincibility, built three flying cities called the Tripura. The cities were engineered in a remarkable way: they all flew in different directions, making them totally impregnable. The only way to destroy the cities was by a single arrow in the brief moment when they were aligned in a single line. Delighted with their invention, the asuras went berserk. They rushed around causing terror and wreaking havoc. They rested secure in the knowledge that it was almost impossible for anyone to defeat them.

The gods turned to Shiva, asking for help against the terror inflicted by the asuras. Shiva mounted a chariot made of the earth. The sun and the moon served as its wheels. The axis of Mount Mandara served as his bow. Adi Sesha, the serpent of time, made up his bowstring and Vishnu himself became his arrow. Shiva was ready to take on the task of destroying Tripura. He followed the three cities for eons, until finally the moment arrived when they were aligned in a single line. In a flash, Shiva drew his bow and let loose his powerful arrow. It found its mark and Tripura, the three flying cities, were destroyed in seconds. Shiva then smeared his body with the ashes of the smouldering cities.

Shiva's bow, made up of space and time, is the symbol of poise, while his arrow, made up of consciousness, is the symbol of focus and concentration. The act of shooting the arrow is no different from the fire-churning of the tapasvin. Both destroy delusions and standards—clearing the consciousness so that it can realise the truth and experience bliss. When the arrow hits its mark, sat-chitta-ananda is attained.

Besides the three bodies we possess, the three cities Shiva destroys also represent the three subjective worlds: the microcosm (the private world), the mesocosm (the social world), and the macrocosm (the rest of the world). They also represent the three objective worlds: the sky populated by gods, the earth populated by man, and the nether world populated by demons.

Shiva is Tripurantaka, destroyer of the three worlds. These three worlds are the worlds we inhabit; the three bodies we possess. Shiva destroys it by churning the fire of tapa and the practice of yoga, represented here as the bow. The archer here is the yogi whose concentration enables him to trascend all things material. This ability to step back and withdraw destroys the material world as it breaks the chain of karma.

The symbols of the number "three" recurring in Shiva's mythology and their possible meanings

Symbols	Possible Meanings
• Three eyes of Shiva	• The aim of tapasya: Sat-chitta-ananda, i.e. Absolute Truth – Purified Consciousness – Perfect Bliss
• Three horizontal ash-lines on Shiva's forehead	• The mundane goals of self-preservation, self-propagation, and self-actualisation (overridden by the spiritual goal of self-realisation)
• Three leaves of the Bilva sprig used in worship	• The three characteristics of matter, inertia, agitation and harmony (tamas, rajas, sattva)
	• The three bodies: physical, mental and causal
• Three blades of Shiva's trident	• The three subjective worlds: the microcosm (the private world), the mesocosm (the social world) and the macrocosm (the rest of the world)
	• The three objective worlds: the sky populated by gods, the earth populated by man and the nether world populated by demons

When the fire of Shiva's tapa destroys the three worlds or bodies, all that remains is ash. Ash is what remains when anything is burnt. Ash cannot be destroyed further. Ash is thus the symbol of the soul, the common indestructible essence of all things that outlives death, and surfaces when external differences dissolve. The soul or spirit is known as purusha in Tantra and as atma in Veda. It is the true identity of all beings, the destination of tapasya. Scriptures believe that the soul is the essence of God. In its realisation lies the state of sat-chitta-ananda.

Shiva smears his body with ash to become Vibhuti-nath, the lord of ash, directing all jivas to look beyond death and differences, towards the soul. The ash is applied to make three lines to remind one of the three bodies and the three worlds that need to be destroyed in the quest for self-realisation. The lines are horizontal to express passivity and inertia, since the only way to truly learn about oneself and one's world is not by reacting to events but by contemplating on them. When the soul is realised, there is no more restlessness. One comes to terms with one's world. There is only peace.

The Vedic yagna also aimed for peace. Hence all ceremonies concluded with the chant "shanti, shanti, shanti". But unlike tapasya, which looked inwards for both peace and divinity, yagna looked outwards. Shiva's fire was churned within the consciousness, while Daksha's fire was churned at the altar. For Shiva, shanti is attained when the mind is purged of all delusions, experiences, and expectations. For Daksha, shanti is attained when nature is reorganized to satisfy one's desires.

Difference between Yagna and Tapasya

Yagna	Yoga-Tapasya
Documented in the Brahmana scriptures	Documented in Aranyaka scriptures
Seeks to appease gods	Seeks God within
Vedic mantras are chanted	Vedic mantras are contemplated upon
Outward-looking	Inward-looking
Involves rituals	Involves austerities
Seeks to change the world	Seeks to change perception of the world
Popular among householders	Popular among hermits
Aligned to social structures such as caste	Rejects social structures
Involves lighting an outer fire	Involves lighting an inner fire
World-affirming	World-renouncing

To Daksha, tapasya was an unproductive, even destructive, exercise. Daksha's primary objective through the ritual of yagna, was to ensure a constant flow of rasa from nature into culture to enrich human life. His hymns and offerings empowered devas to release the life-giving sap hoarded by the asuras. Shiva's fire-churning diverted the flow of rasa away from the cycle of life. As Shiva withdrew heat from the environment into his body, his surroundings became cold and barren —a snow-capped mountain—incapable of nourishing life or sustaining a civilisation. In Daksha's eyes, Shiva was worse than the asuras, who, by converting rasa from organic to inorganic form, were at least part of the cyclical flow of rasa. Shiva's actions worked against the cycle of life. He did not contribute to samsara. He was therefore termed "the destroyer".

Daksha's worldview was populated only with rasa-distributing devas and rasa-transforming asuras. Through the ritual of yagna, he sought to invoke the magical power known as Brahman that would tilt the balance of the cosmos in favour of the devas, enabling them to harvest the world's wealth for the benefit of all jivas. He believed that contentment follows the movement of nature's resources in one's favour. For him, the secret of shanti lay in the control of the world. He sought resolution to the angst of existence through acts of self-preservation, self-propagation, and self-actualisation. This approach to life brought him, and other yagna-performers like him, in conflict with Shiva.

In the following narrative, Shiva communicates the wisdom of life through dance. Just as one can get lost in the outer symbols of a yagna and not realise the deeper meaning of the ritual, one can easily get lost in the beautiful movements of Shiva's dance without realising that there is enlightenment beyond the entertainment. Shiva, who enlightens through dance, is known as Nataraja, the lord of dance. In the narrative, the yagna-performers are identified as followers of Purva-Mimansa. They represent the old school of Hinduism that was ritualistic and focussed on the magical powers of Vedic hymns and Tantrik alchemy. Shiva's dance represents Uttara-Mimanasa, the new school that looked at the meaning beyond the hymn and the ritual. This meaning was not restricted to priests and philosophers but was communicated to the common man through dance and theatre. The dancing Shiva, in effect, represents a revolution that brought cosmic wisdom from the classes to the masses.

ENLIGHTENMENT THROUGH DANCE
[SKANDA PURANA]

A group of sages performed yagna and acquired power from it without appreciating the wisdom inherent in the chants and the ceremonies. To enlighten them, Shiva took the form of a handsome youth and wandered naked into the hermitage of the sages. Such was his beauty that the wives of the sages abandoned their husbands and ran after him. Angry, the sages used the magic of the rituals to create a tiger, a venomous snake, and a goblin. Shiva flayed the tiger alive and wrapped the skin around himself. He caught the snake and wound it around his neck like a necklace. Then, leaping onto the goblin's back, he began to dance. Watching him dance, the sages realised he was God and his dance was a discourse in the meaning of existence. The tiger, the snake, and the goblin represented their desire for self-preservation, self-propagation, and self-actualisation.

What Shiva offered was the chance of self-realisation. In one hand he rattled the drum of death to produce the music of life. In the other he held the flames of destruction that cast the light of learning. Around him emerged a corona cf fire representing the impersonality of nature, the unending merry-go-round of births and deaths. One foot rested on the firmament, within the circle, while the other sought escape. Pointing to the latter, he offered the sages a chance to escape the matrix of delusions and find the truth.

Shiva is Nataraja, the lord of dance. This dance is a visual metaphor of Shaiva philosophy. Every gesture in dance is transitory. It occupies space and time but only momentarily. In his hands is the inner fire of tapa. Around him is the outer fire of samsara. He stands on his right leg and points to the upraised left leg. The left side, because of the beating heart, represents the world which is constantly changing. The right, by contrast, is still like the soul. Shiva tells the observer not to be afraid of the ever-turbulent material world and to focus on the still soul.

The shift from the old ritualistic school of Hinduism to the new theistic school of Hinduism perhaps followed the meeting of two peoples several thousand years ago. The patrons of yagna identified themselves as Arya, "noble", because they had access to the secrets of the Veda. That the yagna did not need a fixed shrine suggests that the Aryas were nomadic herdsmen. As they established themselves in the Indian subcontinent, they came in touch with more settled communities— loosely termed the Dravidas or southerners—who admired hermits and ascetics, masters of alchemy.

As the two groups of people mingled and merged, there was a rich exchange of customs and beliefs. Tensions between the two groups were inevitable. More and more seers questioned the true nature of the Veda and the magic of the Tantra: did the hymns and rituals concern themselves with the workings of the material world or the workings of the mental world? Was Brahman a magical force of the cosmos or merely the dormant divinity within all things?

Those who believed in the former put down detailed instructions of rites and rituals in manuals known as Brahmanas while those who believed in the latter gathered their thoughts in scriptures known as Aranyakas. The dialogues, discussions, deliberations, and debates between the two schools of thought were documented in scriptures known as the Upanishads.

Daksha—the supreme patron of the old ritualistic school—saw Shiva's tapasya as working against the cycle of life. While asuras hoarded rasa, tapasvins diverted the flow of the life-giving sap into the flames of tapa. The withdrawal of energy into the body made the world icy and bleak like Shiva's abode, the snow-capped Kailasa. And the fire within produced nothing but ash that nourished no life. So Daksha refused to patronise asceticism. He forbade offerings in favour of Shiva. The yagna was restricted to gods who harnessed rasa for human society. Unfortunately, Daksha faced opposition within his own family.

DAKSHA'S YOUNGEST DAUGHTER
[SHIVA PURANA]

Daksha offered the gods not only hymns but also his daughters' hands in marriage. His youngest daughter, however, was not interested in any deva. She had given her heart to the mendicant called Shiva, much to her father's dismay. She left her father's side and followed Shiva wherever he went. She became his obedient consort, never questioning his actions, always by his side. She therefore became renowned as Sati, the perfect wife.

Sati, perhaps like many in the Vedic fold, questioned the orthodox ways that gave more importance to the mechanical execution of ceremonies than to the needs of the heart and the questions of the mind. But Shiva's cold detachment from things worldly did not impress her either. She yearned for the middle path where there was husband's love and father's affection.

Sati, the youngest daughter of Daksha, embodiment of the material world, who is determined to draw the indifferent Shiva into worldly life. *Image courtesy: R. G. Singh, Mysore.*

DAKSHA INSULTS SHIVA
[KALIKA PURANA]

Once, Daksha organized a large yagna and invited all the gods to participate. Sati saw the gods and their wives making their way to the patriarch's house. To her great surprise, she and Shiva had been excluded from this elite gathering. Deciding that they had probably been left out erroneously, she decided that she would go. After all, it was her father's house!

Shiva, though, was not so sure that Daksha had actually meant to invite them to his yagna and he expressed this thought to his wife. "No, it must have been an oversight," Sati insisted, unable to accept that her father did not want them to attend his yagna. Seeing Sati's determination, Shiva let her go, preferring to stay where he was. He shut his eyes and went into deep meditation.

Sati reached her father's house. As she entered she saw all the gods gathered there to receive the offerings of the yagna. She swept a glance around the huge pavilion and found that all the seats were occupied. There was no seat reserved for Shiva, her husband! Sati was upset and very angry. She realised that her father had deliberately not extended an invitation to her lord. He had insulted her beloved Shiva. Her fury mounting, she turned questioning eyes upon Daksha. "Your husband is unworthy of any offering," her father calmly retorted. Sati gazed upon her father for a moment, her body trembling with rage, her eyes blazing like burning coals. Then she turned her back upon him and before anyone could comprehend her intention, she leapt into the sacred fire, immolating herself. There was shocked silence in the assembly. The gods looked on in dismay—the sacred precinct had

been polluted and the yagna had to grind to a
halt, leaving it incomplete.

In some narratives, Sati burns herself not by the external fire of her
father's yagna but by the inner fire she kindles by mental concentration.
She thus uses the ascetic route to destroy her father's ritual. The death
of Sati set the stage for a violent confrontation between the world-
rejecting Shiva and the world-affirming Daksha. Shiva experienced
emotions that he never had before. There was loss, pain and rage.
The fire withheld in his body for centuries exploded like a volcano of
emotions taking the form of Virabhadra.

Sati immolates herself when her father refuses to acknowledge Shiva. He
acknowledges only those gods who shower him with material delights. This
burning of Sati stirs emotion in the heart of the indifferent Shiva. He feels pain
and rage. It forces him to react. *Image courtesy: R. G. Singh, Mysore.*

Virabhadra represents the righteous outrage of Shiva against his father-in-law Daksha. Sati's death forces a confrontation between her husband and her father. The husband is shaken out of his indifference. The father is forced out of his avaricious passions. *South Indian temple detail, 20th century.*

SHIVA ATTACKS DAKSHA
[LINGA PURANA]

The news of Sati's death at once reached Shiva at Mount Kailasa. He was devastated. His wife's death broke his heart. His serenity was shattered. And he was enraged. His anger knew no bounds and he went into action. He was intent on taking revenge upon Daksha for the thoughtless action that had led to the death of Sati, his wife and Daksha's own daughter.

In his fury, Shiva pulled out his hair and from that hair, he created a monster—a fanged warrior called Virabhadra, whose sole purpose was to draw blood. Virabhadra rushed to Daksha's house, followed by the ganas, the hordes of ghosts and goblins riding on rabid dogs. The gods were still assembled there, the remains of the yagna strewn around in mute testimony to its abrupt and ill-fated end.

The air was filled with the howl of death as the frightened gods stood by helplessly. Virabhadra and the followers of Shiva went on a bloody rampage. They leapt on the assembled devas, ripping out their hearts and gouging out their eyes. They drank their blood and bedecked themselves with limbs and entrails. The sacred precint of the yagna was transformed into a gory killing field.

Virabhadra then looked around for Daksha, his chosen target. He saw him hiding behind the altar, stunned disbelief on his face. Virabhadra rushed at him, and with one mighty swoop of his axe, he beheaded Daksha. The noble head of the great patriarch was unceremoniously tossed and left lying at the altar. Having destroyed the yagna, Virabhadra returned to Shiva's abode.

Over time, Virabhadra has become the warrior-god who is worshipped by rural communities across India. He is the guardian of the village that is visualised as the mother-goddess by the villagers. *Illustration by author.*

Shiva's followers are known as ganas. Typically, they are visualised as misshapen, corpulent, wild creatures. They represent parts of the subconscious that is repressed or denied. These are released when Shiva's indifference is replaced by righteous indignation.

Sati had brought Shiva in touch with his feelings. In her company he had experienced love. In her absence, he experienced sorrow. Her death made him realise the cruelty of social rules and regulations that often ignore feelings in the quest to establish order. His outrage manifested itself by the overpowering need to destroy the fabric of society itself. His followers, the ganas, spread mayhem wherever they went. They destroyed the yagna, and thus attacked the very foundations of Vedic society.

But the rage and retribution, the destruction of society, did not take away the pain. Shiva clung to Sati's corpse and wandered across the three worlds, howling in agony. His tears turned into sacred beads known as Rudraksha, meaning "from the eyes of Rudra, who is Shiva". The beads thus represent the reaction of Shiva when he finally came in touch with samsara.

SHIVA CALMS DOWN
[VISHNU PURANA]

Virabhadra had killed Daksha. Shiva had his
revenge, but it did not bring back Sati to life.
After destroying Daksha's sacrifice and bringing
death and destruction to the sacred precinct,
Shiva picked up the charred remains of Sati's
body and wandered around the world howling in
agony. The world had become a miserable place,
full of suffering and agony. Shiva could not be
consoled, and bemoaned the loss of his wife.

Shiva, in his indifference, retained all the heat of passion within himself. His
surroundings were therefore still and cold like a snow-covered mountain.
After engaging with Sati, Shiva discovers love and passion. Her death leaves
him distraught. His passion is released. The snow melts. Tears flow.
Illustration by author.

Vishnu was alarmed. He feared for the well-being of the cosmos. Shiva had to stop grieving. Vishnu raised his serrated discus that destroys all negativity, and hurled it in the air. It cut Sati's body into 108 pieces. The physical form of Sati did not exist anymore. With Sati's body gone, Shiva regained his senses. He restored the gods to life and revived Daksha by replacing his cut head with that of a goat.

Daksha completed his yagna and empowered the devas so that the cycle of life could rotate once more. This time an offering was made to Shiva too, at the end of the ritual. Shiva let his dogs consume it. He simply withdrew into a cave, shut his eyes, and immersed himself in his inner world where he re-lit the fire of tapa and destroyed his ties with the outer world.

A modern visualisation of Shiva as one who has regained control of his mind. Calm, composed, withdrawn, he withdraws from the world and retreats into serene isolation after the death of Sati.

Vishnu is that aspect of God that sustains order in nature and culture. While he could understand Shiva's rage against the nature of civilisation, he could not let Shiva destroy society. By destroying Sati's corpse, he was able to make Shiva detach himself from the stimulus of pain. With Sati gone, Shiva was able to overcome his grief and sense of loss. He could even let go of his outrage. He resurrected Daksha by replacing his head with that of a goat and let him continue as before, as the patriarch of Vedic civilisation.

Shiva, however, remained an outsider. He disengaged himself from the world, seeking freedom from those stimuli that cause pain and suffering. Sitting peacefully atop Mount Kailasa, he shut his eyes, withdrew his senses inward, re-lit the flames of tapa, and let his phallus stir in self-containment.

Self-containment invalidates the need for the outer world. Shiva's tapa directs the flow of rasa inward until there is nothing left to rotate the wheel of samsara. The result is entropy, the dissolution of the world. Shiva is therefore Samhara-murti, "the destroyer".

Implicit in the word "destruction" is a sense of something negative. But Shiva's destruction brings peace, or shanti. It leads to sat-chitta-ananda, the state of tranquility when the mind, purged of all delusions, can see the truth. It is the state of God-hood. Shiva, in effect, deconstructs the matrix of delusions that enchants the mind of the jiva leading to yearning and suffering that force him to act and react. Shiva liberates all beings from the fetters of karma.

Tapa destroys karma. It stops the flow of rasa. Without karma and rasa there is no samsara. Without samsara—its turbulence and limitations—the stillness and boundlessness of Brahman make little sense. Just as light cannot be defined unless it is contrasted against darkness, just as the inside of a house cannot be defined unless it can

A 12th century Vietnamese representation of the Goddess who makes a householder of the hermit Shiva.

be contrasted against the outside of the house, the idea of spirit cannot be defined unless it can be contrasted against matter. Unless there is an observation, there cannot be an observer, even one who has shut his eye. Thus the idea of God needs the existence of an equal but opposite: the Goddess.

The Goddess is the embodiment of samsara. She is rasa. She flows. God is Brahman. He is fire—the outer fire of yagna, the inner fire of tapasya. He burns. God is the observer of life while Goddess is the observation that is life. Shiva shuts his eyes to the Goddess because her actions stir emotions in his heart and destroy his peace of mind. Brahma, on the other hand, chases the Goddess and in doing so, he creates the world. This action brings Shiva in direct confrontation with Brahma.

A South Indian bronze image of the Goddess depicts her as being sensous and affectionate. She holds a lotus in her hand. If it is a bud, then she is a virgin. If the lotus is in bloom, then she is a mother.

BIRTH AND BEHEADING OF BRAHMA
[BRAHMANDA PURANA]

In the beginning, on the ocean of milk, within the coils of the serpent of time, Vishnu stirred from his dreamless slumber. From his navel rose a lotus in which sat Brahma. Brahma opened his eyes and realised he was alone.

Lonely, confused, and frightened, he wondered who he was and why he existed. In his quest for answers he went about creating the world. From his mind he moulded four sons, the Sanat Kumars. They were mere boys. They were unwilling to multiply and populate the world. They ran away.

So Brahma created another set of sons, the ten Prajapatis. These were willing to multiply but did not know how. So Brahma split himself into two. From his left half emerged a woman called Ushas, the dawn. As soon as Ushas appeared before Brahma, Brahma experienced an insatiable sensory thirst that needed to be quenched. Overwhelmed with yearning, Brahma lunged at his daughter, desperate to unite with her. She ran away from the incestuous gaze of the father, taking the form of various beasts: cow, mare, goose, and doe. He pursued her, taking the form of the corresponding male: bull, horse, gander and stag.

The sons of Brahma realised that the father was doing what he should not do. They cried out in disgust. Out of their cry emerged Rudra, the one who moans, a terrifying archer who shot an arrow and pinned the father to the sky.

A fundamental principle guiding Hindu thought is that nothing exists unless it is perceived by a conscious being: there is no observation without an observer. This makes the idea of "awareness" or "consciousness" central to Hindu thought. Thus, God destroys the world by shutting his eyes as Shiva. God creates the world by opening his eyes.

The period "before the beginning" does have a sentient being in it—Vishnu. But he is in a dreamless slumber—unaware of himself or his surroundings. This unawareness is "nothingness" in the Hindu worldview, a period of irrelevance, a time called pralaya or dissolution when both the observer and the observation are formless, like the placid "ocean of milk". All that remains, perhaps, is time—represented by the coiling and uncoiling serpent whose name Adi-Sesha, primal-remainder, or Ananta-Sesha, endless-remainder, draws attention to the idea that time remains both *after* the world comes to an end and *before* it re-emerges.

The waking up of Vishnu, the blooming of the lotus, the birth of Brahma, his first set of four sons, and his second set of ten sons, represent the quickening of the consciousness and the evolution of the mind. The mind evolves because Brahma seeks to understand his true nature and identity. If Brahma had no questions, if Brahma felt complete, if Brahma had been totally self-contained, he would never have "looked" for answers: the observer would have had no observation, and life would never have been "created".

That the first four mind-born children of Brahma are called "ancient", yet visualised as pre-pubescent boys, indicates that they are four aspects of the primal mind—the discriminating intellect and the three containers of experiences, desires, and learning—before the mind was exposed to any sensory stimulation. Their lack of sexual maturity suggests that they have no knowledge of, or desire for, external stimulation. They are in a state of sat-chitta-ananda and have no wish to shatter this primal purity. Hence they disappear soon after birth.

The next ten mind-born sons of Brahma are the five sense organs (eye, ear, nose, tongue, and skin) and the five response organs (face, hands, legs, anus, and genitals). They are the channels that connect the mind to the external world. But the presence of organs that can sense and react are useless without a source of stimuli and a destination for responses.

The world is created by Brahma who is born of Narayana. This is a visual and narrative expression of the Hindu belief that the world is a creation of consciousness. Narayana represents consciousness that is asleep. Brahma is consciousness that is awakened. *Illustration by author.*

In the Hindu creation myth, all characters are male up to this point. Then comes the girl child. Her name, Ushas, means "the dawn" because her arrival marks the dawn of life. Life happens only when matter stimulates the mind. In Hindu symbolism, male forms have been used to depict the intangible inner realities of life while female forms have been used to depict the tangible outer realities of life. Only when Brahma acknowledges the outer world can he begin his journey to explore his inner world. She, the embodiment of matter, is the non-self, without whom Brahma's self cannot be defined or distinguished. She is thus the personification of Brahma's world, Brahmanda. She is the object, he is the subject. She is the observation, he is the observer. She is the source of stimuli, the destination of responses, the fountainhead of experiences, desires, and learning. She is the Goddess.

Two sides of reality

	The Divine Within	The Divine Without
Meaning	Consciousness	Manifestations
Mythological gender	Male	Female
Tantrik terminology	Purusha	Prakriti
Vedic terminology	Atma	Maya
Nature	Spiritual	Material
State	Still	Ever changing
Form	Spirit	Substance
Metaphysical qualification	Subject	Object
Metaphysical role	Observer	Observation

The Goddess is Brahma's "daughter" because the existence of the material world presupposes the existence of a sentient being who is aware of the material world. Brahma, the observer, must exist before Ushas, the observation. It is his motivation that leads to her discovery, hence creation. She is supposed to answer his questions about himself. But at this point, something else happens.

The awakening of Vishnu is pre-determined by the fact that he did go to sleep. What follows—the rise of the lotus from his navel, the birth of Brahma, his primal question, the creation of his sons and his daughter —seems orchestrated; it lacks spontaneity. This changes the moment Ushas appears. Brahma's reaction is not spontaneous. It is a choice. Ushas was created out of Brahma's desire to know himself. By desiring to possess her, he abandons this primal quest. His attention shifts from discovery of the inner world to the conquest of the outer world. The response Brahma chooses, arouses disgust. It is "incestuous".

Instead of "learning" from the daughter, he seeks to "copulate" with her. Ancient seers thus linked a spiritual outrage with a social judgment.

Ushas' transformations are not spontaneous. They are induced by Brahma's "incestuous gaze". Thus the transformations of the world are determined by the perceptions of the observer. Since the law of karma dictates that every action must have a reaction, the first transformation induced in matter by Brahma's desire leads to subsequent transformations. The fleeing Ushas metamorphoses into a cow, a mare, a goose, a doe. Because of her transformations, she comes to be known as Shatarupa, she-of-infinite-forms.

Watching the primal jiva losing himself as he seeks to possess rather than learn from his daughter, the sons of Brahma are horrified. They realise that Brahma's actions will pollute the chitta, distort vision of sat, and take away ananda. They seek someone who will prevent these mental modifications. So they call for help. Shiva appears as Pinaki, the archer. He shoots the arrow and pins Brahma to the celestial sphere, just as he once shot an arrow to destroy the three cities.

The deer is the symbol of the restless mind. In art, Shiva is shown holding a deer in his hand. He calms it down. The bow used to do so represents tapasya. In the centuries that followed, tapasya became popular as yoga. The term yoga has its roots in the Sanskrit verb yuj which means "to yoke". Yoga is all about bridling the mind so that it stands firm, unaffected by the world. Shiva has yoked his mind and his semen (and that of Brahma) by purifying his consciousness, shattering all delusions, and realising unconditional bliss. Shiva is therefore known as Yogeshwara, lord of yoga.

In the pursuit of his daughter, Brahma forgets the original purpose of creating her. Rather than using her as the medium to reflect on his identity, he begins adopting new and false identities—becoming the male complement of every female form she takes. These are mental modifications, the gradual acquisition of memories, desires, learning, and finally, the ego, that take Brahma away from Vishnu. In the following narrative, the dance of matter enchants and influences the mind so that the one head of Brahma becomes four, then five. But none look below towards the reclining Vishnu: the inner self, the Vedic atma, the Tantrik purusha.

Shiva is the lord of yoga, hence Yogeshwara. Yoga is the method by which the mind can be liberated from the snare of the outer material world. It is the process by which the crumpled consciousness can be uncrumpled. Shiva holds a deer in his hand, which represents the restless mind. Yoga puts this deer-mind at ease.

BRAHMA'S FIFTH HEAD
[SHIVA PURANA, NARADA PURANA]

Such was Brahma's desire for his daughter when she circumambulated him that he sprouted four heads, facing the four cardinal directions, so that he could look upon her at all times. When she flew skywards, he popped a fifth head on top of the other four. This display of unbridled passion disgusted Prajapati's children. They cried. In response, Shiva took the form of a terrifying being called Bhairava, who wrenched off the fifth head of Brahma. Thus sobered, Brahma began to sing the four collections of Vedic hymns, each emerging from one of the four remaining heads.

Bhairava represents the most fearsome form of Shiva. In his hand he holds the fifth head of Brahma which is the ego that deludes the mind, entraps it in the material world, and ensnares it away from the soul. *Wall painting from Rajasthan.*

47

The link between man and woman is desire, as is the link between the internal self and the external non-self. This makes life an affair between the Brahma, the divine within all sentient beings, and the Ushas, the divine without. Ushas is Shatarupa as she appears in myriad forms. Ideally, she should be Vidya, the goddess of knowledge, helping Brahma know himself. Instead, swept away by the transformations of the world, failing to realise that each of her forms is merely a projection of his own experiences and expectations, she becomes Maya, the goddess of delusion. The father who creates the daughter ends up being controlled and contorted by her. He comes to possess three more heads. And finally the fifth head—the ego.

Allegorical counterparts of Metaphysical Concepts

Metaphysical Concepts	Mythological Characters	Gender
Unmanifest Consciousness (the spirit)	Vishnu	Male
Mind's capacity to discern and distinguish things	Brahma	Male
Mind's constituents: the intellect, and the containers of experience, desire, and learning	Four Sanat Kumars	Male
Mind's inward and outward channels: five sense organs and five response organs	Ten Prajapatis	Male
Fifth head of Brahma	Ego	Male
Material world, the source of stimuli and destination of responses, the external matrix	Ushas	Female

The fifth head rests atop the other four. Implicit in the upward orientation of the head is arrogance born of ignorance, just as the downward orientation of the head implies humility born of wisdom. The fifth head looks skywards, away from Vishnu. It takes Brahma away from the goal of existence, which is self-realisation.

The narrative clarifies that the ego has no independent existence like Vishnu. It needs the "daughter" for its creation. The ego validates its existence by seeking control of, and acknowledgement from, the material world. When neither is forthcoming, there is suffering.

A cycle of yearnings and frustrations comes into being. Freedom from this endless, meaningless cycle is possible only when the false identity, the ego, is completely destroyed. This is what Shiva does as Bhairava.

Bhairava means "he who evokes terror". Bhairava represents the terror of life, the endless anxiety and uncertainty that threatens existence when the mind is dominated by the ego. In this form, Shiva severs Brahma's fifth head to become Kapalika, the bearer of the skull. Shiva uses the skull to drink the nectar of sat-chitta-ananda.

South Indian illustration of Shiva as Kapalika, the bearer of Brahma's skull. Brahma's obsession with the material world filled the world with passions and desires and restlessness that angered Shiva who yearned for stillness and serenity.

In many narratives, the pillar of fire does not emerge from Shiva; Shiva emerges from the pillar of fire.

A South Indian temple image of Shiva emerging from a pillar of fire, the linga, that has no beginning or end. Brahma took the form of a swan but could not find its top. Vishnu took the form of a boar but could not find its base. Without beginning or end, this pillar of fire was a visual form of God.

THE PILLAR OF FIRE
[SHIVA PURANA]

Brahma, the father of sentient beings, and
Vishnu, the upholder of cosmic order, both
claimed to be the creators of the world.
Suddenly there appeared before them a pillar of
fire. It seemed to have neither a base nor a tip.
Brahma took the form of a swan and rose into
the sky, but could not find its tip. Vishnu took
the form of a boar and burrowed into the earth,
but failed to find its base. The pillar had neither
base nor tip, neither a beginning nor an end,
neither an origin nor a destination. It seemed
self-created, self-sustained, and self-contained.
Brahma and Vishnu concluded that this pillar of
fire was greater than the two of them and all
the gods put together. It was the symbol of a
great god or Maha-deva. It was the symbol of
the ultimate form of the divine. From this pillar
emerged Shiva. Both Brahma and Vishnu saluted
Shiva and sang songs in his praise.

The narrative visualises Shiva not only as the supreme tapasvin but
also as the embodiment of tapa and the final goal of sat-chitta-ananda.
Shiva is not merely the fire-churner. He is the fire. He is not simply the
God-seeker. He is God.

Beyond the allegory is a clear sectarian tilt. As ancient Hinduism, which
was rather agnostic and ritualistic, transformed and became more
theistic, God was visualised in three ways: Brahma, Vishnu, and Shiva.
The priest-like Brahma was associated with the God accessed through
mechanical rites known as yagna, the king-like Vishnu was the God
approached through the devotional and emotionally-charged ritual of
adoration known as puja, while the hermit-like Shiva was the God
realised through intellectual ascetic practices such as tapasya. These
became the three tributaries of Hinduism.

There was great conflict between the followers of the three forms of God and the superiority of one over the other often expressed itself through narratives. For some, the answer to life lay in rituals. For others, it came by adoring God in temples. And then there were those who believed that all answers lay in meditation and contemplation.

While the approach varied, the goal of all these paths was the same: the intention was to realise God. For through God, in God, one obtains that eternally elusive state of shanti or peace.

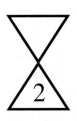

SEDUCTION OF SHIVA

The hermit finally marries the Goddess and engages with the world

2

SEDUCTION OF SHIVA

The world exists because sentient beings perceive it and respond to it. With each reaction, rasa is spent. Every time rasa is spent, it flows. As rasa flows, samsara blooms, and the wheel of existence turns.

Shiva does not react. He does not spend rasa. He withholds it. He shuts his eyes, bridles his senses, and refuses to perceive the world. The world around him therefore ceases to be. There is no flowering or fruition. Shiva's abode is therefore a mountain of ice. Cold. Lifeless.

While Shiva churned the inner fire of tapa, the gods looked forward to the outer fire of yagna which empowered them in their battles against the asuras. Each time they won, rasa gushed out of earth's every pore: rivers flowed, plants bloomed, rocks melted to release metal, and mountains cracked to spill out gems. The earth became bountiful, her wealth displayed in all its splendour for the world to see.

But while the gods could release and redistribute the earth's treasures, they did not have the power to regenerate them once spent. That power rested with the demons. The asuras knew how to bring the dead to life. They could rejuvenate the earth and restore its fertility. They could replenish subterranean stores of water and minerals. All thanks to Shukra, lord of the planet Venus, the guru of the asuras, who possessed the science of renewal known as Sanjivani Vidya. Shukra obtained the secret lore of the Sanjivani Vidya from none other than Shiva himself.

Shukra is the lord of the planet Venus associated with intuition, sensuality, and creativity. He is called Kavi, the poet. He is the guru of the asuras, and has only one eye, unlike Brihaspati, lord of the planet Jupiter, guru of the devas. Shukra thus represents the instinct and emotion which lacks the balance of intellect and rationality, represented by Brihaspati. Shukra is the keeper of Sanjivani Vidya or the science of regeneration. He can regenerate the subterranean asuras after they have been cut down by the devas during harvest time.

SECRET OF REGENERATION
[MAHABHARATA]

The devas continued to perform yagnas to gain strength. The hymns chanted during the performance of the yagnas empowered them. With this recharged power the gods were able to slaughter the asuras and win every combat.

The yagnas were always performed to gain advantage for the gods. No one performed yagna favouring the asuras. The balance of power was therefore heavily tilted in favour of the gods and the asuras needed to find some way of overcoming them. Finally, Kavya-Ushanas, guru of the demons, turned to tapasya. By lighting the inner fire of tapas, he hoped to overpower the outer fire favouring the gods. He undertook severe ascetic measures to achieve his aim. He hung himself upside down from the branch of a tree over a raging fire, breathing nothing but smoke for a thousand years. When these austerities reached their climax, Kavya-Ushanas came face to face with Shiva. Shiva opened his mouth and swallowed Kavya-Ushanas, trapping him within his body. Kavya-Ushanas tried to escape but found that Shiva had closed all his orifices, all except the penile passage. As Kavya-Ushanas slipped out of this aperture, he came to possess all the knowledge associated with renewal, regeneration, and reproduction.

Kavya-Ushanas' journey through the body of Shiva made him realise the interdependence of tapa and rasa. Just as Shiva transformed rasa into tapa by withholding it in his body, tapa could be made into rasa by causing it to flow outwards. Shiva's inner fire was thus a vast reservoir of energy into which anyone could tap to restore life on earth. To acknowledge Shiva as his teacher and father, the eternal and exhaustible source of life-giving energy, Kavya-Ushanas took on the title of Shukra, "the seed", keeper of fertility. With this science of regeneration, Shukra was able to revive asuras killed in battle. The asuras, in turn, were able to recreate plant and mineral wealth that the devas could draw and distribute, but never generate. This is why in art Shiva is always shown surrounded by demonic, asura-like, frightening beings. In his presence, they are ganas, minions of God.

But while asuras knew how to transform tapa into rasa, the asuras did not share their wealth with the world. When they were powerful, the earth was barren. The Aryas therefore despised them as niggardly hoarders. By performing yagna they empowered devas, who released rasa hoarded by asuras. Hoarded rasa nourished no one. Hoarding was therefore a crime. Daksha, patriarch of Aryas, opposed Shiva for withholding his semen. He admired Indra for shedding his semen freely. He even cursed Chandra, the moon-god, with the wasting disease because he refused to share his semen with all his wives, thus behaving as a hoarder no different from an asura.

Shiva gives refuge to the moon in the locks of his hair. Mere contact with Shiva helps the waning moon wax. Shiva is thus the source of infinite power. He is no ordinary god. He is God.

WAXING OF THE MOON
[SOMANATH STHALA PURANA]

Daksha was the father of many daughters. He gave twenty-seven of his daughters in marriage to Chandra, the moon-god, who was renowned for his beauty and virility. Each of Daksha's daughters was a nakshatra, or lunar mansion. Of all the nakshatras, Rohini was the most beautiful and alluring. Chandra preferred the beautiful Rohini to his other wives and found himself seeking her out more than the others. His other wives felt neglected and complained to their father who threatened Chandra with dire consequences if he did not treat all his wives with equal affection as was expected of any polygamous man. Chandra, however, disregarded Daksha's threat and continued to love the beautiful Rohini to the exclusion of his other wives. Daksha's threat took effect and Chandra was cursed with a degenerating disease.

As the days passed, the moon-god lost his potency, and began to wane. Terrified, he did not know what to do. Finally, he took refuge with the only god who had opposed Daksha— Shiva. He housed himself on Shiva's head. There, he found the power to regenerate himself: his potency returned and he began to wax. With joy and gratitude he addressed Shiva as Chandra-shekhara, saviour of the moon. A sobered Chandra thereafter decided to devote one night to each of his twenty-seven wives. He waxed on the days that he approached Rohini and waned on the days that he moved farther from her. On the new moon night he had no wife by his side. On the day before, when he was just a crescent, the moon celebrated Shiva-ratri, the night of Shiva, and took refuge in Shiva's locks, safe in the knowledge that he would have the power to regenerate and wax again.

Chandra, the moon god, is visualized as riding an antelope in Indian scriptures. In Nepalese paintings he rides a chariot that is drawn by geese. The waxing and waning of the moon represents the constant change of moods that stabilise by resting on Shiva who is God. *Illustration by author.*

The restoration of Chandra made the devas realise what Shukra had already known: that Shiva's tapa could nourish life too. Just as Shiva drew on the rasa of the outer world to light the inner tapa, the outer world could sustain itself by drawing energy from Shiva. Clearly, Shiva was no mere ascetic-god of the Dravidas. He was not merely the teacher of yoga and tapasya. He was much more than an alchemist.

He was the embodiment of the Brahman invoked in the yagna. Worship of Shiva was no different from performing yagna. This realisation caused Vedic society to abandon ritualism in favour of theism. The fire altars were abandoned and shrines were built where Shiva was adored as Mahadeva, the greatest of gods, God. The asuras worshipped him because a passage through Shiva's body revealed the science of regeneration to their guru. The devas worshipped him because he helped the waning moon wax by simply placing Chandra on his head.

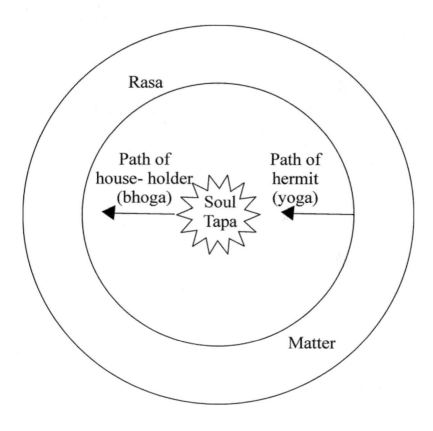

Fire can be spent interacting with the outer world of rasa or retained by withdrawing into the inner world. The former process is called bhoga while the latter is called yoga.

The asuras were not content with being restored to life by their guru. They wanted to defy death and control the flow of rasa. To do this, they began performing tapasya and lighting the inner fire of tapa—just like Shiva.

But Shiva performed tapasya to burn the fetters of conditioning and throw light on the true nature of things. His aim was sat-chitta-ananda. His goal was samadhi, liberation from samsara. The aim of the asuras' tapasya, however, was siddhi, manipulation of samsara by unlocking the mysteries of rasa. The asuras accumulated tapa, not to burn the fetters of worldly life, but to control the substance of the cosmos in order to hoard wealth and survive any onslaught of the devas.

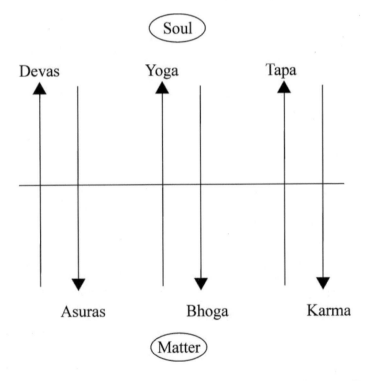

Devas and asuras represent the force and counterforce of nature. Devas draw rasa upwards, out of the earth. Asuras withdraw rasa downwards, into the earth. The action of the devas draws the earth's bounty towards man. Hence, they are deemed gods. The hoarding asuras are rejected as demons.

A BOON FOR TARAKA
[SHIVA PURANA]

Once, an asura named Taraka was desirous of
attaining power to be able to defeat the gods
and control the world. He decided to perform
tapasya to achieve his goal. He sat still,
completely absorbed in his penance, refusing to
react to any worldly stimuli, with no thought of
time. Such was his concentration that God
appeared before him in the form of Brahma. "What
boon do you seek Taraka?" asked Brahma.
Taraka's single-minded pursuit was to acquire
siddhis and material gains that would enable him
to be master of all he desired. Rather than use
the moment to liberate himself from the cycle
of rebirth, Taraka asked Brahma to make him
immortal. When Brahma firmly replied that that
was not possible since all living organisms must
eventually die, Taraka asked for a boon that
would make him almost immortal. "If I must die,
let it be at the hands of a child who can fight
battles when he is six days old, on the seventh
day of his life." Brahma granted him his wish,
adding that such a child would only be a son of
Shiva.Taraka was satisfied. Empowered by this
boon, he went about his mission with zeal. He
drove the gods out of the celestial realms and
became master of the three worlds.

The triumph of Taraka led to cosmic chaos. Wealth was regenerated
and hoarded, not distributed. It was time for the gods to assert
themselves. But the gods did not know how. No yagna was powerful
enough to produce such a hyper-masculine warrior-child. According
to Tantra, a child is born when the white seed of man mingles with the
red seed of woman during the fertile period. The biology of the child
conceived depends on the power of the respective seeds. A male
child is conceived when the white seed is powerful and a female child
is conceived when the red seed is powerful. When both red and white

seeds are equally powerful, the child is neither male nor female. Asceticism and continence make a seed powerful, sometimes so powerful that it does not need the support of a red seed or the warmth of a womb. Since Shiva was the greatest tapasvin, who had remained continent for eons, the gods concluded that his seed was the most powerful of all, capable of producing the hyper-masculine warrior-child who could kill Taraka. Energized by tapas, Shiva's semen moved upwards. It was time to make Shiva's semen move downwards and produce a child out of it. It was time to make Shiva a father.

So they invoked the Goddess. She was once Sati who had provoked Shiva into action. Though she had died, they believed they could resurrect her like all things material and make her enchant Shiva again. She was Yoga-nidra, formless and unobserved when consciousness was withdrawn. She was Yoga-maya, full of forms when consciousness gave her attention. Goddess worship became part of the Hindu mainstream centuries after the nomadic Aryas settled in the Indian subcontinent. In early Vedic scriptures, there are references to goddesses such as Aditi, the mother of the devas, and Prithvi, who embodies the earth. But these female deities are reduced to insignificance by their male counterparts such as the thunderous rain-god Indra, the effulgent fire-god Agni, and the radiant sun-god Surya. In later Vedic scriptures, female deities play a more central role. Like the ascetics, the goddesses perhaps made their entry into Hinduism after the Aryan tryst with the Dravidas.

That yagna, the primary Vedic ritual, did not demand a permanent shrine suggests that the animal-herding nomads were not as rooted to the soil as the Dravidian communities, who in all likelihood were farmers tuned to the rhythm of fertility. The latter saw the earth as the Goddess who nourished living things with milk, demanding nourishment of blood in return. This Goddess had two mutually dependent forms—the docile, loving, maternal aspect called Mangala-Gauri and the wild, bloodthirsty, killer aspect called Chandika-Kali. The former was given flowers and incense; the latter was offered blood through animal sacrifices.

The Goddess who creates life also destroys life. As Gauri, the mother, she gives milk but as Kali, she stretches her tongue to drink blood. *Poster art from Bengal, 20th century.*

With the mingling and merging of Aryan and Dravidian worldviews, the Goddess had been acknowledged by the Aryas as Sati, the daughter of a yagna-performing Daksha and the consort of a tapasya-performing Shiva. Both relationships were fraught with tension: the father sought to control the daughter, the husband preferred to ignore the wife. She was the battleground where the world-affirmer and the world-rejecter met and clashed.

A Mithila painting showing Kali striding on the indifferent Shiva.

As Sati, the Goddess had forced Shiva to feel and respond to worldly stimuli. Then she had died, childless. As the embodiment of all things material, the gods were sure they could make the Goddess return once again and make Shiva open his eyes. Because of her transformations, she came to be known as Shatarupa, she-of-infinite-forms. Since her forms were enchanting and deceptively unchanging, she was called Maya, the embodiment of delusions. She was also Shakti, the energy, whose form was determined by the gaze of the observer. She was Prakriti, nature, the individual's world. She was Saraswati, the medium of enlightenment, as well as Lakshmi, the source of nourishment.

Ushas, Shatarupa, Maya, Shakti, Prakriti, Saraswati, and Lakshmi are all titles of the Goddess. Brahma "creates" her by becoming aware of her. This may not be entirely true. For when Vishnu sleeps, the world continues to exist albeit in a dissolved state as the ocean whose waters serve as Vishnu's bed. Only Vishnu is not aware of this Goddess-bed. Since Hindu seers were concerned with subjective, not objective, worlds, for them awareness of the Goddess was pre-requisite to her existence. For Goddess-worshippers, the Goddess exists always: when Vishnu is asleep and when he is awake. When Vishnu is asleep, when consciousness is not sensitive to life, the

Goddess exists as Yoga-nidra, the great slumber. When Vishnu awakens, when consciousness is sensitive to experience, the Goddess exists as Yoga-maya, the great delusion that is life. When there is enlightenment, Vishnu experiences the Goddess as Yoga-vidya, the wisdom of experience.

Brahma, Vishnu, Shiva are all manifestations of God. In Hindu mythology, the term "God" indicates the divine within while the term "Goddess" represents the divine without. God "creates" the Goddess by becoming aware of her. The Goddess enables God to realise his God-hood. Thus, in her, he is truly born. This explains the Vedic verse: "Out of God was born Goddess and out of Goddess was born God."

In narratives, Saraswati is said to be Brahma's consort, Lakshmi is Vishnu's consort and Shakti is Shiva's consort. Thus God cannot exist without the Goddess. In other words, the inner subjective world cannot exist without the outer objective world. Brahma cannot create anything without Saraswati, who is knowledge. Vishnu cannot sustain anything without Lakshmi, who is wealth. Shiva cannot destroy anything without Shakti, who is power. The symbol of man and woman, and their mutual interdependence, helped ancient seers explain with great simplicity complex ideas of interdependence of concepts. It was impossible to explain the concept of "subject" without the concept of "object" just as it was extremely difficult to explain the concept of "man" without the concept of "woman". And so it came to pass that man came to represent subject and woman came to represent object. He was intangible spirit; she was tangible matter.

Bronze image of the head of the Goddess placed on pots and baskets during worship. It indicates that the Goddess is the container of all that is eaten. She sustains life on earth. She is the mother.

The Goddess stepping on the male head representing the ego which deludes the mind into believing it can control and dominate the world. She holds in her hand a sword and a vessel full of the blood of those who seek dominion over her. She is the embodiment of nature that can never ever be tamed. *Poster art from Kerala.*

Of course, one may wonder why the male form was associated with the still, serene, permanent soul, and the female form with the ever-changing, restless, permanent matter. Perhaps the seers saw in the regular transformation of the female body, in the menstrual tides, a link with the regular transformation of nature—the waxing and waning of the moon, the rising and ebbing of tides, the change of seasons. This made the female biology, which created life within itself, more suitable to represent ideas of fertility and worldliness, whereas the male biology, which created life outside itself, was more suitable to represent ideas of monasticism and otherworldliness.

The Goddess took birth as Parvati, the daughter of the mountains. Her father was Himavan, god of the Himalayas, the great snow-clad mountain range that borders India's northern frontier. He was the king of all the mountains. And like all mountains, he represented stability and permanence. Shiva meditated on these mountains. So great was Shiva's tapasya that all the heat was absorbed into his body, making the mountains cold and devoid of life. It was up to the daughter of the mountains to bring life into this barren, desolate landscape.

At first, she tried seducing Shiva, making herself beautiful and presenting herself before the ascetic as a nymph. This trick had worked with other ascetics. Whenever the gods had seen an ascetic perform tapasya, they had sent down a nymph to seduce him. The nymphs always succeeded in making ascetics shed seed and stay rooted to earth.

MENAKA'S CHARMS
[MAHABHARATA]

Sage Vishwamitra was born King Kaushika. One day, marching at the head of his troops, he reached the ashram of the sage Vashishtha, where he was warmly received. Vashishtha was the owner of a celestial cow called Kamadhenu—the one who fulfills all desires—and was able to extend hospitality and satisfy every request made by the king. Kaushika was overtaken by envy and greed. He wanted to possess the wonderful cow but the sage refused to part with it. Thereupon, Kaushika used force to try to acquire the cow but his army and weapons were no match for Vashishtha's spiritual powers. The defeated Kaushika decided to undergo penance and obtain supernatural powers.

He spent years in meditation, finally gaining the power he sought. His years of penance transformed him and he decided to give up his kingdom and live the life of an ascetic. As sage Vishwamitra, he churned the fire within and became so powerful that the gods were afraid. Indra, king of the gods, decided to send the nymph Menaka to distract Vishwamitra and seduce him. Menaka was an apsara, beautiful and voluptuous. She danced before Vishwamitra, flaunting her charms, finally forcing him to open his eyes and submit to her.

Nymphs in Hindu mythology are known as apsaras. The word has its roots in apsa or water. They are embodiments of rasa. They make the world go round by drawing energy out of tapa and channelling it towards samsara. Nymphs are thus the water that puts out the fire of tapa. The water-nymph is thus in eternal conflict with the fire-ascetic. While he seeks to withdraw from the world, she seeks to draw out tho ascetic. She is the womb that seeks to milk the seed out of the body so that it can rotate the cycle of life. She is the obstacle to tapasya, the greatest enemy of the tapasvin.

Symbolism of Fire and Water

Fire	Water
Tapa	Rasa
Masculine	Feminine
Inner Reality	Outer reality
Spirit	Matter
Shiva	Shakti
Hermit	Nymph
Phallus	Womb
Staff	Pot
Pestle	Mortar

If indifference is the path that ignites tapa, then desire is the tool to make rasa flow. "Desire," proclaims the Rig Veda, "transforms the unmanifest idea, asat, into the manifest form, sat." The world becomes manifest and life begins only when the individual desires to know his true self. So says the Upanishad. To know the self, the individual needs to know what the self is not. For without perceiving the other, one cannot distinguish and establish oneself. To perceive the other, one must open his eyes and let energy flow in the direction of samsara. To make Shiva open his eyes and interact with the world, the gods summoned Kandarpa, the love-god, the lord of sensory arousal.

13th century image of Kandarpa from Belur, Karnataka, shows him holding his sugarcane bow and flower arrows. He arouses the five senses and fills the heart with desire.

This is how the scriptures describe Kandarpa: a winsome dark god, who rides a parrot, who wields a sugarcane bow whose bowstring is made of bees, who has five flowers serving as his five arrows with which he arouses the five senses. His companions are gandharvas and apsaras, who are fairies born of the perfume and nectar of flowers. They dance and sing, serenade and seduce, as he shoots his merry arrows. Rati and Priti, the goddesses of erotic craving and emotional yearning, are his consorts. They ride mynah birds and hold aloft his banner, which carries his symbol, the zodiac Capricorn known in Sanskrit scriptures as makara. Every year when the sun enters the house of makara, it is spring. The time of love and longing. Of flirtation and romance. Of birds and bees. But Shiva holds him in disdain and looks upon him with a fiery glance.

THE FIERY GLANCE
[SHIVA PURANA]

The asura Taraka, empowered by Brahma's boon, was creating havoc. He unleashed terror in all the three worlds. The gods were alarmed. They realised that Taraka was invincible. The only way to annihilate him was to get Shiva to procreate a son. The gods decided that his beloved Sati had to be reborn as the daughter of King Himavat. Thus was born Parvati, with the mission of marrying Shiva and begetting a son to put an end to the menace of Taraka.

Time went by and a young, beautiful Parvati went to Shiva's abode and began to tend to him. However, in spite of all her efforts she was unable to attract his attention. In despair, the gods asked Kandarpa to enchant Shiva, make him open his eyes and shed his seed. Kandarpa's presence filled the air with romance: Shiva's snow capped mountain transformed into a pleasure garden full of flowers, bees, and butterflies. Flowers bloomed to greet Kandarpa, they made offerings of pollen and nectar at his feet. Nymphs danced, while fairies sang, cheering Kandarpa who raised his sugarcane bow, drew his bowstring of bees and shot five arrows at Shiva. The arrows stirred the yogi's senses. He was not amused. He opened his third eye and let loose a fiery missile that set Kandarpa ablaze and reduced him to ashes. Having destroyed the lord of sensory-indulgence, the lord of sensory-discipline resumed his meditation.

Shiva had no interest in the cycle of renewal. He was blissfully immersed in tapasya when Chandra took refuge on his head and when Shukra passed through his body. The benefits that the two deities derived from their contact with Shiva were purely incidental. Shiva remained an indifferent outsider. If anything, Shiva opposed the fertility cycle.

Parvati, princess of the mountains, sought to win the heart of the ascetic Shiva, with a little help from Kandarpa, the love-god. But they failed miserably. With his third eye, Shiva destroyed desire. He wanted nothing. Not even the love of Parvati. *Image courtesy: R. G. Singh, Mysore.*

To Shiva, the unending transformations of nature brought anticipation and frustration with unfailing regularity. They reminded him of the joy he felt when Sati danced on his lap and the misery he experienced when he held her corpse in his arms. To him, the world was merely a matrix of delusions that took the mind away from the state of sat-chitta-ananda. So he severed all association with the material world, shut his eyes, withdrew into cold, dark caves and meditated on sterile snow-clad mountains, warming himself with the inner fire of tapas.

When Shiva opened his third eye and destroyed the love-god Kandarpa, it was clear to the gods, and to the Goddess, that Shiva was no ordinary ascetic who could be seduced. He had to be forced to abandon his ascetic ways through a display of unshakable resolve and absolute devotion. So the Goddess decided to make Shiva open his eyes, not as a nymph, but as a hermit.

According to Hindu metaphysics, since all creatures—animate and inanimate, temporal and divine—are linked by karma, it is possible to change the course of life by introducing one's desire into the cosmos. Desire has to be introduced with stubbornness until the cosmos has no choice but to yield and give in to one's wishes. This is hatha yoga or the yoga of unshakeable resolve. Unshakeable resolve was expressed through acts of austerity and self-mortification. It was not mere meditation or contemplation. Sometimes it involved giving up food, sleep and comforts, and sometimes, outright torture—sitting on fire, sleeping on thorns, or standing on one foot with upraised arms.

Parvati's actions are different from Shiva's. Shiva's meditation is an expression of indifference to worldly life; her austerities are an expression of her determination to have her way. He lights the inner fire, one that burns everything around. Parvati uses the accumulated energy to force an event around her. She creates a stimulus to which Shiva has no choice but to respond. It is not a stimulus that enchants Shiva. It is a stimulus that demands his attention.

Shiva's third eye is oriented neither to the left nor to the right. It indicates non-judgemental awareness. Shiva rises above the need to classify the world as good or bad, right or wrong, appropriate or inappropriate. He is thus beyond love and hatred. This ability, to transcend the world and be non-judgemental, enables Shiva to destroy Kandarpa, god of desire, with the fire of ascetic indifference. *Illustration by author.*

A detail from a South Indian temple showing Parvati determined to become Shiva's wife. Since he refuses to submit to desire, she appeals to him through penance. She is determined to make him part of the world. And she displays her determination by submitting to various ordeals such as standing still in cold water. This display of determination forces Shiva out of his indifference. It forces Shiva to care for the world. It makes the hermit a householder. It transforms Shiva into Shankara.

PARVATI WINS SHIVA'S HEART
[SHIVA PURANA]

To help Parvati the mountain-princess win the heart of Shiva, the gods had enlisted the help of Kandarpa but Shiva reduced him to ashes by a single glance of the third eye. Parvati, however, continued to visit Shiva's cave every day with a basket of food and flowers. She cleaned the cave and took care of the ascetic but he remained totally indifferent to her affection. Determined to marry the stubborn hermit, Parvati eventually left her father's house and took to living as an ascetic in the forest. She withdrew into herself and withheld all thought, action, breath, and seed. So great was her tapasya that it threatened the foundations of the mountains. In the wake of such determination, Shiva was forced to open his eyes. He tried to dissuade Parvati, informing her that life with a hermit would be nothing like the life she had with her royal father. He suggested she marry a prince or a god, someone young and handsome and virile. But Parvati would not budge. She was adamant. Shiva was forced to acknowledge that he had met his match. He agreed to marry Parvati. Bent on making a householder of this hermit, the mountain-princess insisted he marry her in the ritually prescribed manner.

In India, women seeking good husbands emulate Parvati. On particular days of the week such as Monday, associated with the moon-god and Shiva, they fast in the hope of getting the husband of their choice. This fasting is called vrata or observance, an abbreviated form of Parvati's penance that enables one to get what one desires. A vrata is a personal ritual, not one that is performed by priests. It involves not just ritual acts but also complete focus of the mind and the heart on the desired result. Vrata is considered to be a ritual act through which one can manipulate the workings of the cosmos. It is an internalized yagna.

The aim is not to change one's view of the world but to change the world itself.

Shiva opened his eyes and agreed to be Parvati's groom. But there was a problem. Shiva did not know the rules of social conduct—what was considered appropriate or inappropriate, what was auspicious and what was inauspicious.

A Mysore painting showing Shiva as Sundereshwara, the beautiful one, who is to be Parvati's groom.

THE HIDEOUS GROOM
[LINGA PURANA]

In the sacred scriptures, it has been stated that the groom must come to the bride's house with his family and seek her hand in marriage. Shiva, the ascetic, had no family, so he invited his companions to his wedding. To the horror of the gods, the retinue comprised ghosts, goblins, gnomes, witches, vampires, and dwarfs. Shiva himself rode a bull. He smoked hemp and drank poison. His companions, who did not know the ways of the world, bedecked him with ash, skulls, bones, serpents, and animal hide. When he arrived at the gates of the mountain-king's palace, the women who had assembled to welcome him ran away in fright. Mena, Parvati's mother, refused to accept this man, who looked like a beggar and resided in crematoriums, as her son-in-law. Parvati pleaded with Shiva, "You promised to marry me. Please take the form that pleases my parents, at least until they have given consent to our marriage." So Shiva let the gods bedeck him as they deemed fit. Shiva was bathed with celestial waters and dressed in silks, flowers, gold, and gems. When the gods had finished, he looked more handsome than Kandarpa himself. He was as fair as the full moon. His limbs were as lithe as those of a dancer. All the assembled women fell in love with him. They declared him Sundareshwara, the lord of beauty. Even Mena was impressed. Joyously, she let Shiva marry her daughter. In the presence of the gods, in a ceremony presided over by Brahma himself, Shiva and Parvati exchanged garlands to become husband and wife.

This is Shiva's second marriage. In both weddings he was the reluctant groom. In the first, he married the daughter of Daksha, the primal priest. In the second, he married the daughter of Himavat, the mountain-king. In the first, he annoyed his father-in-law when he did not bow to him. In the second, he scared his father-in-law when he appeared dressed as a beggar and mendicant. In the first, the Goddess had merely walked out of her father's house to marry Shiva. In the second, the Goddess had insisted that Shiva come to her father's house to claim her. There is a conscious effort by the Goddess to bring together the patrons of yagna and the followers of tapasya through love and understanding. For both aspired to peace, one by churning the outer fire and the other by churning the inner fire. The Goddess finds merit in the path of the priest-kings who seek to establish a peaceful society as well as the path of hermits who seek an inner peace. She bridges the gap between the outer way and the inner way. With bhakti-yoga, the path of devotion and understanding, she unites karma-yoga, the path of action, and gyana-yoga, the path of introspection. The heart succeeds in uniting mind with matter.

Types of Yoga

Gyan	Bhakti	Karma	Hatha
Head	Heart	Society	Body
Intellectual	Emotional	Social	Physical
Philosophical	Devotional	Duty bound	Penance
Understand the nature of all things around	Unconditionally love the nature of things around	Respond to things around with detachment	Express determination through action to change the nature of things

In the southern traditions, Parvati is described as Vishnu's sister. Vishnu is the keeper of cosmic and social order, the upholder of natural and cultural values. He is the champion of the gods, who ensures the rotation of the cycle of life. He knows that this marriage of Shiva with Parvati will result in the birth of children who will ensure that Shiva's power becomes part of the world, not indifferent to it. Their children will kill demons, remove obstacles, and bring material prosperity. In art, he is shown as giving the Goddess' hand in marriage to Shiva.

Kalamkari print showing Shiva taking his bride to his mountain retreat on his bull Nandi.

In Tantra, Shiva is visualised as a white, ashen corpse with an erect penis. He is so internalized that his body does not sense the outer world—it is like a dead body. His semen flows upwards, lighting the inner fire of inner wisdom, born by deconstructing the outer world. The flames leap up and stir his phallus. The Goddess appears in the form of Kali, who is dark, bloodthirsty, naked with unbound hair—sexual and violent simultaneously. She cuts her own head and drinks her own blood, indicating her autonomy. At the same time she sits down to copulate with Shiva, indicating her dependence. By copulating with Shiva she is forcing him to acknowledge the outer world where matter manifests in various forms. She seeks to draw out his energy, his semen. Her womb is the pot of life-giving water. By sitting on Shiva's phallus, she encloses the fire of the inner world with the waters of the outer world.

In South Indian temples, the Goddess is shown as the sister of Vishnu, the worldly form of God, who gives his sister to Shiva, the ascetic form of God. The Goddess is the world that is protected by Vishnu, as brother, and witnessed by Shiva, as husband.

A more abstract representation of the sexual union is the Shiva-linga enshrined in Hindu temples. If one takes away the body of the copulating Shiva and Shakti except for the genitals, what remains is an upward pointing phallic shaft of Shiva who lies on his back surrounded

In Tantra, the Goddess is visualised as copulating with Shiva by sitting on top of him. Shiva's state of self-contained bliss is likened to a corpse or shava with an erect phallus. The Goddess, as Kali, who embodies unfettered sex and violence, transforms the "shava" into "shiva" by forcing the corpse to awaken and engage with the world. *Popular Bengali brass art.*

by a leaf-shaped trough, the lips of the Goddess' vagina. Thus the devotee stands within the womb of the Goddess. The entities around are manifested forms of rasa. Life happens when the Goddess tries to draw God into the world, transforming his world-denying fire into her world-sustaining sap. The pot hanging on top of the linga in Hindu temples is yet another representation of the yoni of the Goddess. The water hopes to douse the flames of Shiva's fire and transmit its energy into the material world.

In geometry, the union is depicted as the union of the downward-pointing triangle (the womb) with the upward-pointing triangle (the phallus). The six-pointed star indicates the union of Shiva and Shakti.

Just as man without woman serves no purpose, Kali and Shiva have no purpose independent of each other. She is matter, he is soul. By forcing Shiva to unite with her, Kali draws Shiva into the material world. She gives the soul purpose. He gives matter value. Modern illustrations downplay the explicit sexual metaphor. *Poster art.*

It is a geometric depiction of the Shiva-linga, with the upward-pointing triangle representing the shaft of the linga and the downward-pointing triangle representing the yoni-trough. These geometrical representations of metaphysical ideas are known as yantras.

In Goddess worship, autonomous forms of the goddess such as Kali are represented by downward-pointing triangles without the upward-pointing triangle. This is reinforced by several such triangles, one within the other. When the Goddess is visualised as a mother, her yantra includes both the upward-pointing and downward-pointing triangles, such as in the Shri-yantra.

The sexual act was more than just a sexual act to the seers. In its simplest form it was the union of man and woman, an act of fertility. The meanings transcended biology and evolved with the seeker's understanding of the world .

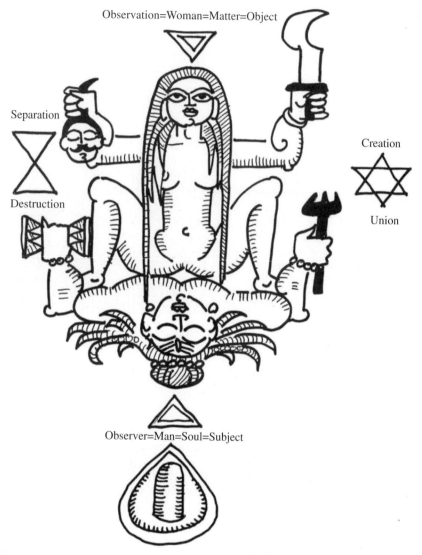

Observation=Woman=Matter=Object

Separation

Creation

Destruction

Union

Observer=Man=Soul=Subject

Disembodied linga-yoni with woman on top

Shiva's linga worshipped in temples is enclosed within the yoni of the Goddess. It represents matter drawing consciousness into the world. Shiva is outside. The Goddess brings him inside. By engaging with the Goddess, by observing the world, he will know who he truly is. *Illustration by author.*

The Goddess, as Kamakshi, holding in her hands the symbols of Kama or Kandarpa: the sugarcane, the flower, the parrot, and the pot. She sits on Shiva and forces him to engage with the world. *Illustration by author.*

The damaru or rattle drum of Shiva is an artefact modelled on two triangles separated from each other. The triangles represent man and woman, inner and outer reality, soul and matter, subject and object. When separated from each other, there is destruction. *Illustration by author.*

Layers of meaning within the Linga-Yoni symbol

Linga	Yoni
Phallus	Womb
Manliness	Womanliness
Spirit	Matter
Soul	Substance
Seed	Soil
Brahman	Samsara
Inner Reality	Outer reality
Divine Within	Divine Without
Intangible Divine	Tangible Divine
Tapa (spiritual fire)	Rasa (material sap)
Mind	Matter

Skanda. *Ilustration by author.*

The gods wanted a hyper-masculine child to kill Taraka; they wanted a being who was ageless so that even on the seventh day of its life, when it was six days old, it was powerful enough to fight the demon. In other words, they wanted an embodiment of tapa that was not bound by the rules of samsara. They wanted the Goddess to milk out Shiva's seed but not nurture the seed in her womb. So they charted an elaborate plan to prevent the red seed of the Goddess from mingling with the white seed of God.

BIRTH OF SKANDA
[VAMANA PURANA, SKANDA PURANA]

The gods interrupted the lovemaking of Shiva and Parvati. Embarrassed, Parvati turned away and Shiva's semen spurted out. The fire-god Agni caught the semen in his flames but found its radiance too powerful to bear. To cool it down, he gave the seed to Vayu, the wind-god, who, having failed in this endeavour, plunged it into the icy waters of the river Ganga. The river water started to boil, such was the energy contained in Shiva's seed.

Six forest-virgins, the Krittikas, wives of the seven celestial sages, who were bathing in the river, became pregnant with that one seed. Their husbands declared them unchaste. In shame, they cleared their wombs and abandoned the unborn foetuses in Saravana, the forest of reeds.

No sooner did the foetuses touch the ground than the forest of reeds was set ablaze. In the forest fire the six foetuses united to become one child with six heads. The Krittikas wanted to kill this child as he embodied their shame. But as soon as they came near him, their breasts started oozing milk. Overcome by maternal affection, the Krittikas nursed this child whom they named Kartikeya, the son of the Krittikas.

The child born of Shiva's seed that had been milked by Parvati and incubated by Agni, Vayu, Ganga, and Saravana and nursed by the Krittikas, was also named Skanda. When Skanda was six days old, on the seventh day of his life, he was strong enough to pick up a lance and lead the gods into battle against Taraka. After a fierce fight he triumphed over Taraka.

Shiva's son, born of his seed, but incubated in many wombs such as fire, wind and water, is the lord of the planet Mars. He is known by many names such as Kartikeya, Murugan, Skanda, Kumara. He is the god of war, of aggression, the commander of the army of the devas. He embodies that aspect of Shiva that has become part of the world following the efforts of the Goddess. *Popular art.*

Thus, through Skanda, Shiva participates in worldly affairs. In art, Skanda is represented by symbols of masculinity such as the lance, the rooster, and the peacock. He is associated with the planet Mars. Skanda is popularly worshipped in South India as Murugan, the boy-god, and as Kumara, the eternal child. He is Subrahmaniam, the helpful god, who stands atop mountains and protects mankind. He has two consorts: Sena, the daughter of the devas, and Valli, the daughter of local tribes. According to some, his wives are symbols of his army and his weapons to whom he is married. In North India, he has no consorts. He is a virile war-monger who takes men to battle and makes widows of women.

But the Goddess is not satisfied with this offspring of Shiva. He had been neither nurtured in her womb nor nursed on her breasts. Though this child of Shiva had helped the world, he did not represent Shiva's direct interest in worldly events. Shiva remained as indifferent as ever. The marriage had been forced on him. Even their lovemaking, with her on top, seemed one-sided. His semen had spurted out rather unintentionally. While the gods had got their champion, the Goddess wanted more from Shiva. She wanted him to truly father a child and through him, contribute to the workings of the world.

A 12th century representation of Ganesha from Belur, Karnataka, shows him as a corpulent elephant-headed being. His body is created by the Goddes but his head is given by Shiva. Thus, he personifies the union of Shiva and the Goddess.

BIRTH OF GANESHA
[SHIVA PURANA]

Parvati wanted Shiva to father a child. But he refused. An exasperated Parvati created a child on her own using the turmeric paste she anointed herself with. The child was called Vinayaka because he was born without the intervention of a man. One day, Parvati asked her son to guard the entrance to her bath and not let anyone in. Vinayaka obeyed, blocking even Shiva's entry, not knowing he was his mother's consort. An otherwise detached Shiva lost his cool, raised his trident,

and beheaded the stubborn lad. Parvati was inconsolable in her grief and threatened to transform from Gauri, the life-giving goddess, to Kali, the life-taking goddess, if her son was not resurrected. Shiva therefore ordered his followers, the ganas, to fetch him the head of the first living being they encountered. They brought back the head of an elephant, which Shiva placed on the severed neck of Parvati's son and restored him to life. By giving him life, Shiva became the boy's father. He acknowledged his fatherhood by naming the lad Ganapati, lord of the ganas.

13th century representation of Ganesha from Vietnam.

Parvati's fury at the death of her child forces Shiva to act. When he resurrects her creation and appoints him as leader of his followers, he consciously becomes father and thus part of the material world. The resurrected Ganapati, with a body created by the Goddess and a head given by God, represents the transformation of Shiva, the hermit, into Shiva, the householder.

The choice of an elephant's head is interesting. In Hindu symbolism, the elephant represents material abundance. Indra, king of the gods, rides an elephant. Elephants flank Lakshmi, the goddess of wealth and prosperity. Shiva, who rejects material pleasures, is described as Gajantaka—he who flays the elephant and uses its thick skin as his upper garment. By using the elephant's head to resurrect the child of his consort, Shiva, in effect, demonstrates his participation in the world of rasa. He uses the power of tapa to bring to life the child he killed. Ganapati's head represents tapa; his body represents rasa. He reconciles God and Goddess. He becomes the doorway through which Shiva enters samsara.

A South Indian bronze image of Shiva as Gajantaka, the elephant killer. Elephants represent the bounty of the world that Shiva is indifferent to. That he uses the head of an elephant to resurrect the son of Parvati indicates his involvement in the material world.

Although living with his wife and two children, Skanda and Ganapati, Shiva is a reluctant householder. He does not find material life to be meaningful. Though the Goddess manages to make him a father, she finds it difficult to make him a true householder. He does not appreciate the meaning of a home.

North Indian miniature showing Shiva with his family. Shiva is the only Hindu deity to be shown with his wife and children. This is interesting since Shiva is a hermit god. For a hermit to be depicted as a householder repeatedly draws attention to the eternal conflict in India between householders who enjoy the world and hermits who renounce the world.

A HOUSE FOR PARVATI
[FOLKLORE]

Parvati once begged Shiva to build her a house. "Why do we need a house?" Shiva wondered. In summer when it is hot, I sit under the shade of the Banyan tree. In winter, when it is cold I warm myself in the crematorium beside funeral pyres. In the rainy season, I simply fly and sit on the clouds above the rain.

Parvati suffers her husband's idiosyncrasies, taking care of her children on her own. She becomes Gauri, the radiant mother, who takes care of her household without any help or support from her husband. In India, women worship Gauri as she represents marital resilience.

INFIDELITY
[FOLKLORE]

Parvati often fought with Shiva because he never paid attention to his children. He withdrew constantly, either meditating or smoking cannabis. She was left to fend for the family all by herself. Once, tired of her constant nagging, Shiva went to the pine forest. Parvati followed him there, taking the form of a tribal girl. Shiva began to miss Parvati. He pined for her. Suddenly, he realised he was being watched by a tribal girl. She reminded him of Parvati. Overwhelmed by desire, he chased the girl and forced her to make love with him. The girl laughed, then cried, then revealed her true identity and accused Shiva of infidelity. Shiva tried to reason with her but she was inconsolable. To calm down, Parvati decided to bathe in Lake Manasarovar. When she returned to the banks, she discovered that mice had chewed her blouse. To her delight, a tailor was passing by. He agreed to darn her blouse if she paid him for it. "But I am the wife of a penniless hermit," she said. "In that case, pay me with an embrace," said the tailor. Parvati agreed. When the blouse was darned, the tailor demanded his payment and Parvati obliged. After they had made love, the tailor burst out laughing. It was none other than Shiva. "You are no different from me," he said. "I am," she cried. "You were unfaithful because of lust. I was unfaithful because of poverty."

From time to time, however, the Goddess ensures Shiva knows her value as the following narrative shows.

The Goddess as Annapoorna or Gauri, she who serves food, is worshipped at Kashi. At Kashi the snow melts to form the river Ganga. At Kashi there is life and death. Kashi is different from Kailasa. There Shiva is without the Goddess. All around him there is stillness and snow. There is neither life nor death. This benevolent form of the Goddess, also known as Mangala or Bimala, contrasts the blood-drinking, terrifying form of the Goddess as Kali or Chandi. *Illustration by author.*

ANNAPOORNA'S KITCHEN
[KASHI STHALA PURANA]

Once, Shiva said that he did not need a consort. So Parvati walked out of Mount Kailasa. Some time later, Shiva felt hungry. At such times he usually went to Parvati. But this time she was not around. And there was no food in the kitchen. The hunger pangs became unbearable with the passage of time; Shiva could neither meditate nor sit still. Desperate, he wandered through the three worlds in search of food. As the days passed he realised the value of the Goddess, how she sustained the body in the jiva's quest for self-realisation. When he heard that Parvati had set up a kitchen in the city of Kashi he rushed there with his begging bowl. He apologized and requested her to feed him. She filled his bowl with food and he ate to his heart's content. Shiva declared Parvati to be Annapoorna, the goddess of food, and took her back to Mount Kailasa so that she could set up her kitchen on its icy slopes.

Gauri, the maternal form of the Goddess. *Poster art.*

According to one narrative, Shiva was so pleased with Parvati when she fed him that he embraced her tightly, so tightly that his left half became one with the Goddess. This gave rise to the form known as Ardhanareshwara.

While Shiva is often visualised as half a woman, the Goddess is never shown as half a man. This is because the Goddess represents matter. She is the object. She is the observation. She is passive. Action has to be taken by the observer, the subject, the soul, represented in art as male. *Illustration by author.*

BHRINGI CURSED
[TAMIL TEMPLE LORE]

Bhringi was a devotee of Shiva so he wanted to circumambulate the lord but not his consort. "We are two halves of one," said Parvati who sat on Shiva's left lap and prevented Bhringi from going around Shiva alone. Bhringi took the form of a flea and tried to fly between their heads. Parvati fused her body with that of Shiva so that she became Shiva's left half. Bhringi then took the form of a worm and tried to bore between the two halves of Shiva's body. Angered by his refusal to acknowledge her, Parvati cursed Bhringi. "You shall lose all those parts of the body that come from a woman," she shouted. Instantly, his body was stripped of flesh and blood. He was left with nothing but bones and nerves. Bhringi collapsed on the floor and realised he could not even stand. He understood the value of the Goddess. To remind him and others like him that Shiva was incomplete without his consort, Parvati refused to restore his body to its original state. Instead, Shiva gave Bhringi a third leg so that he could stand like a tripod.

Shiva's purity balanced with Shakti's pragmatism balances the world order. He is the Truth, free of restrictive definitions. She is the Reality, where space and time give the world name and form and determine what is spiritual and what is material, what is appropriate and what is inappropriate. She takes his seed into her womb and transforms the mystery of the divine into tangible manifestations of wealth and wisdom, brains and brawn.

Bhringi tried to deny the value of the Goddess hence was stripped of his flesh and blood. To stand erect he begged Shiva to give him a third leg of bone. *Illustration by author.*

Children of Shiva and Shakti in Bengal Iconography

Deity	Gender	Appearance	Nature	Role
Lakshmi	Female	Wife	Restless	Grants Wealth
Saraswati	Female	Spinster/ Widow	Serene	Bestows Knowledge
Ganesha	Male	Scholar/Priest	Clever	Removes obstacles
Kartikeya	Male	Warrior	Mighty	Kills demons

Durga

Lakshmi

Saraswati

Ganesha

Kartikeya

Durga, the most worshipped form of the Goddess, embodies the world that has been domesticated. Unlike Kali, whose sexual and violent nature is unbridled, her sexual and violent side is domesticated to the benefit of society. She is a wife and mother. She kills to defend and to feed. When domesticated, the world brings forth her children—wealth, knowledge, brain, and brawn.

The Goddess sits beside Shiva and tempers his innocent ways so that it helps society. She introduces divisions and standards into his vision. She makes him appreciate the divide between the seer and the scenery, the subject and the object. When his innocence lands him in trouble, she works hard to rectify the damage.

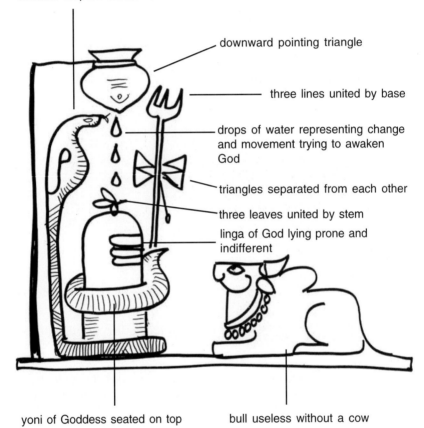

hooded serpent indicative of stillness

downward pointing triangle

three lines united by base

drops of water representing change and movement trying to awaken God

triangles separated from each other

three leaves united by stem

linga of God lying prone and indifferent

yoni of Goddess seated on top

bull useless without a cow

Decoding of various elements that constitute Shiva's shrine. The aim is to symbolically represent various elements that make up Shaiva philosophy. *Illustration by author.*

GRACE OF SHIVA

*The hermit becomes the accessible and benevolent
householder called Shankara*

Shankara and his family. *Poster art.*

3

GRACE OF SHIVA

With the Goddess by his side, Shiva is no longer indifferent to the woes of the world. His eyes are open. He sees, he listens, he reacts. His radiance nourishes samsara. Devotees acknowledge him as Shankara, the source of joy; as Shambhu, the abode of joy; and as Ashutosh, the one who is easy to please.

Water is poured on the Shiva-linga to draw out the energy of Shiva's tapa visualised as the erect phallus. Through it, Shiva's grace reaches his devotees. *Image courtesy: R. G. Singh, Mysore.*

A LEAF FROM A THIEF
[SHIVA PURANA]

The thief was not so lucky this time. The villagers had laid a trap for him and nabbed him red-handed. He managed to escape their clutches somehow, but they gave chase, determined to teach him a lesson. They chased him through the village and across the fields, all the way into the forest. He finally managed to throw them off his trail by hiding in the dense, dark undergrowth.

But his troubles were not over yet. He had barely caught a breath when he heard a low, ferocious growl. Soon he was on the run again, this time being chased by a hungry beast. His legs were beginning to give away underneath him and he scrambled up a tree to escape the hungry jaws that were snapping at his heels.

All night long he stayed up there in that tree, afraid to sleep in case wild animals climbed up and made a meal out of him. When he heard them prowling beneath the tree, he shook the branches vigorously, hoping that would scare them away.

What he did not know was that he had climbed a Bilva tree that had a linga installed under it. As he shook the branches, the Bilva leaves fell in a gentle shower onto the linga. Moreover, that night was the thirteenth night of the waning moon and all the gods and the demons were invoking Shiva, as was the custom.

Unknowingly, the thief too was making offerings to the Lord, by showering the linga with Bilva leaves. That was enough to please the Lord and earn him a place in his heart.

According to Ayurveda, the Hindu science of health and healing, Bilva is a coolant. Its leaves transform Shiva's tapa into rasa that seeps into the material world as his grace. Bilva leaves are also believed to be the physical symbols of the Goddess' love for Shiva.

North Indian miniature painting. Women worship the Shiva-linga on Mondays to get a good husband of their choice, just as the Goddess got the husband of her choice.

LAKSHMI'S BREAST
[ORIYA FOLKLORE]

Lakshmi, the goddess of wealth and prosperity, once decided to make an offering of a thousand tender lotus buds to Shiva. The gods in the heavens were impressed by her devotion but they were also keen to know how far she would go to keep her pledge. They decided to put her to test and ensured that she found only 999 lotus buds. Try as she might, Lakshmi could not find just the one additional bud that would complete her offering.

Now, Lakshmi was a picture of beauty and grace, with many a poet having sung her praises. She recalled how one of them had described her breasts as tender lotus buds. Determined to keep her promise at all costs, she offered one of her breasts to the Linga. Shiva was deeply moved by her devotion and transformed her breast into a round and succulent Bilva fruit. He declared that henceforth, he would not accept any prayer unless it was accompanied by an offering of Bilva sprigs.

The Bilva leaf offered to Shiva is considered a form of Lakshmi, the goddess of worldly fortune. It is supposed to cool the fiery Shiva and bring his grace into the lives of devotees.

Lakshmi is a form of the Goddess. She is visualised as a golden nymph, bedecked in red silk, gold, pearls, and diamonds, who holds in her hand the pot of bounty and sits on a lotus. According to folk traditions of Bengal, she is the daughter of Parvati. Her husband is none other than Vishnu, the more worldly form of God. Vishnu brings peace to the world and Lakshmi brings prosperity. By accepting Lakshmi's breast as an appropriate offering, Shiva reaffirms his grace to the material world.

An image of the Shiva-linga from Vietnam, with the breasts of the Goddess making the trough.

Shiva also supports Vishnu in his quest to establish dharma in the world. Shiva gives Vishnu his most feared weapon, the Sudarshan Chakra. When Vishnu incarnates as the priest, Parashurama, it is Shiva who teaches him the martial arts so that Vishnu can kill all the unrighteous kings who populate the earth. Legend has it that Parashurama taught the martial art known today as Kalaripayattu to Nair warriors of Kerala. Nair warriors, in turn, taught it to Buddhist monks who travelled to China and transformed it to the now popular martial art called Karate.

In many parts of India, village-guardians and village-heroes such as Mallana of Andhra Pradesh and Khandoba of Maharashtra are considered to be local manifestations of Shiva. With Shiva participating in worldly affairs, the common man saw Shiva as a guardian god. He became renowned as Vireshwara, lord of the brave, protector of the weak, and destroyer of villains. In the epic Mahabharata, warriors such as Drupada and Arjuna invoke Shiva to destroy enemies and procure weapons.

Folk gods such as Mallanna and Khandoba are seen as forms of Shiva who guard the village from predators.

THE PASHUPATA MISSILE
[MAHABHARATA]

The Pashupata missile contained the power of a thousand wild beasts. It was no wonder then that Arjuna, the greatest of warriors, coveted the missile. His armoury was incomplete without it. Firm in his resolve to obtain it, he installed a Shiva-linga of sand and began to invoke Shiva. He was the picture of concentration and devotion as he sat there, day and night, breathing the name of the Lord. The gods were impressed with his determination and they hoped Shiva would grant him the boon he sought.

One day, a wild boar wandered close to the Shiva-linga, snorting and grunting as he foraged for food. Arjuna was enraged at this intrusion. Reaching for his bow, he shot the boar down. When he approached the stricken beast though, he was surprised to find that two arrows had pierced its body. As he stood there perplexed, the wife of a tribal warrior came up, claiming it was her husband's arrow that had killed the boar. She also claimed that the boar's tusks were theirs by right.

Arjuna was incensed. He refused to part with the animal and challenged the tribal warrior to a fight. His opponent was more than a match for him and apparently had boundless energy as well. He bounced back from every blow that Arjuna struck, ready for more. Arjuna now began to tire. In desperation, he grabbed some wild flowers and threw them on the Shiva-linga that he had been worshipping. Instantly, he was energised and he rushed to challenge the tribal warrior afresh.

He froze in his tracks, however, when he saw that the flowers he had thrown at the linga were on the head of the warrior. It was then that he realised that the warrior was none other than Shiva himself and his wife was the Goddess Parvati. Throwing his bow down, he bowed to Shiva, with great humility and respect. Shiva was pleased with his devotion and his valour. "You are truly a great warrior. You are worthy of possessing the Pashupata," he said.

This narrative views Shiva as a tribal hunter and links Shiva with forest dwellers, people who were considered by the Vedic priests to be lowly outcastes because they did not value the rules of the yagna. It reflects the period when Shiva, the outsider god, was slowly being accepted within the Vedic pantheon. The distant mendicant, shunned by Daksha's Vedic priests, eventually became the patron of Vedic warriors. He wanted no elaborate chant or ritual, just sincere devotion expressed through simple offerings.

Shiva is often associated with hunters. Perhaps long ago he was the lord of the hunt, to be propitiated because he was also Pashupati, lord of the beasts.

AN EYE OF THE HUNTER
[PERIYAR PURANA]

Deep in the forest was a cave with a linga. Everyday, a priest made his way to the cave and worshipped at the shrine. In the forest, there lived a hunter called Kanappan, who was a Shiva devotee too. Unlike the priest, who made his offerings in the manner prescribed in the scriptures, the hunter always offered the Lord the choicest part of his game.

The hunter was ignorant and illiterate. He had no knowledge of the purification rites nor was he aware that certain acts would pollute his offering. As his hands were full of the game that he had killed, he carried the water for the offering in his mouth and the flowers on his head.

Neither the priest nor the hunter wavered in their devotion to the Lord. The gods, watching from the heavens above, were intrigued by these two and wondered which one of them was the greater devotee. Shiva decided to put them to the test.

One day, as they entered the shrine, the two devotees found that the linga had sprouted two eyes. They could not contain their joy, for it could only mean that the Lord wanted to see them. Their delight soon turned to horror, however, as one of the eyes began to bleed. The priest cried out in terror and ran away, convinced it was a bad omen.

The hunter was distraught at the sight, believing his Lord to be in pain. He ran into the forest, gathered some medicinal herbs and placed them on the bleeding eye. But they were of no use and the eye continued to bleed. The hunter could not bear the sight and decided to transplant his own eye onto the linga. Using his knife, he carved out one eye and fixed it on the linga. No sooner had he done that than the other eye began to bleed. The hunter did not hesitate even for a second. He decided to carve out his other eye too. Placing his foot on the linga so he would know exactly where to fix the second eye, the innocent devout cut his second eye out.

In that instant, Shiva appeared before Kanappan and clasped him to his heart, assuring him of a place by him forever.

In many parts of India the Shiva-linga is encased in a metal mask with the face of a virile, moustachioed man on it. Clearly, not everyone was pleased with the aniconic (and phallic) symbol of Shiva. They wanted Shiva to possess a form: that of a virile warrior.

Shiva's association with low-caste people and his disregard for formal ritual made him popular among the masses. In narratives, his devotees came to include ghosts, goblins, gnomes, vampires, witches, and other wild spirits, shunned by all. Shiva's entourage of ganas is described as an unruly and rowdy bunch of wild ogres who obtain true unconditional acceptance from Shiva. He drinks with them, smokes with them, and never gets annoyed with their rather antisocial behaviour.

This is perhaps why Shiva became the patron deity of hippies and flower children in the 1960s. He gave space to all non-conformists. He accommodated all those who did not fit in. The ganas were so fond of their lord that they happily did whatever he told them to do without question.

Mysore painting of the Nayanar sage Kanappan who cut out his eye for Shiva.
This is an expression of passionate and violent devotion that had its roots in
South India around the 5th century BC.

KIRTI-MUKHA
[LINGA PURANA]

One of Shiva's hordes, the ganas, wanted to eat the asura Rahu. When the gods heard of this, they ran to Shiva and pleaded with him to stop the gana somehow. "Rahu is critical to preserving the order in the universe, Lord! He is one of the nine astrological bodies that determine the influence of time on destiny. Please save him from the hungry gana!"

Shiva agreed to intervene. Summoning the gana into his presence, he forbade him from eating Rahu. "But I am hungry, Lord! I must eat something," the gana pleaded. "Eat yourself," was Shiva's curt reply.

The gana did not stop to think. Without any hesitation, he began eating his own legs, his arms, his trunk...until all that was left of him was his head. Shiva was moved by this display of total obedience. Praising the gana he said, "From now on, your face will be atop pavilions, gates, and entrances. You are Kirti-mukha, the face of glory. You will look into everyone's heart and mock the pretenders. You will scare away those that are unwelcome."

Shiva's devotees include ganas like Vyaghra-pada, he-of-the-tiger-feet, who, when offered a boon, begged for tiger feet so that he could walk through the forest and collect Bilva leaves for his lord without worrying about thorns and sharp stones. There is also Kubera, the king of yakshas, and the rich treasurer of the gods who sometimes needs to be taught a lesson.

FOOD FOR GANESHA
[HIMALAYAN FOLK TALE]

Shiva, the ascetic, had become a householder after marrying Parvati. Though he was devoted to his family, his ways had not really changed. And it upset Parvati enormously that he did not provide for his children. They went hungry often and Parvati would fight with Shiva about his indifference to their plight.

Kubera watched the goings-on and felt sorry for his Lord. One day, he visited Parvati and offered to feed Ganesha at his own house. Parvati's face flushed with humiliation, but Shiva did not notice anything amiss. Ganesha was delighted at the prospect of a good meal and Parvati eventually allowed him to go.

Kubera ordered an enormous meal for Ganesha. It was wolfed down in no time and Ganesha asked for more. He attacked his second helping with enthusiasm and again asked for more. This went on till they had run out of supplies in the kitchen and even in the palace storehouse. But still Ganesha's hunger was not satiated.

Kubera was not to be outdone, though. He spent vast sums of money and had food delivered from all the corners of the world. Ganesha gladly ate it all. And still he asked for more.

Soon Kubera had emptied his treasury and he was in tears. "I have nothing left to offer," he wept, humbled by poverty. "Oh," said Ganesha, his elephant face beaming in a wide grin, "this is just like my father's house."

An enlightened Kubera bowed to him as he realised that no amount of material wealth can truly satisfy hunger.

Like ganas and yakshas, Shiva's devotees include rakshasas and asuras. In the Vedic scheme of things, rakshasas were demons because they followed the law of the jungle and asuras were demons because they were niggardly hoarders of cosmic bounty. Shiva is unable to judge his devotees as gods or demons. He simply responds to sincere devotion, much to the irritation of the devas.

Kubera is the king of the yakshas, who are guardians of treasures and visualised as corpulent misshapen beings. He is associated with a mongoose that spits out gems. He rides not on an animal but on humans. He is the lord of the northern direction. *Illustration by author.*

MOVING KAILASA
[RAMAYANA]

Ravana, the king of the barbarians, was a ferocious enemy of the gods. With ten heads and twenty arms, he could see and attack in all directions. But like so many others, he too craved the favour of the Lord.

One day, he cut off one of his heads and one of his arms, to fashion a lute. Using the head as a resonant gourd, he fixed the arm on it, plucking the nerves to make divine music. He played this lute everyday, singing the praises of Lord Shiva.

Shiva was moved by his devotion and appeared before Ravana. "Ask what you will and it shall be granted to you," he said to the demon king. "There is nothing more precious to me than you, my Lord. I want you to reside permanently in my kingdom," replied Ravana. Shiva agreed, much to Ravana's delight. He picked up Mount Kailasa and headed south, to his island kingdom of Lanka.

The gods watched these developments in horror. They knew that with Shiva by his side, Ravana would become truly invincible. If Ravana acquired the power to rule the world, it would spell doom for the gods. He had to be stopped somehow. The gods sought the intervention of Varuna, the god of the sea.

As Ravana was transporting Mount Kailasa to his kingdom he felt his bladder filling up. The pressure became so enormous that he was afraid he would soil himself. He just had to put the mountain down and run into the bushes to relieve himself. In that moment his devious plan was foiled and the abode of Shiva was restored to the Himalayas.

Shiva's boons make demons powerful. But his sons, especially Skanda, lead gods in their battle to overpower demons and liberate cosmic bounty. The tension between the force and counter-force of nature rotates the wheel of life. In the following narrative, Shiva helps a powerful barbarian king and creates anarchy on earth. To repair the damage, the gods need the help of Vishnu.

No temple of Shiva is complete without an image of Ravana holding up Mount Kailasa. Ravana, king of the rakshasas, was so arrogant of his strength that he thought he could carry Kailasa home. Shiva stopped him by pinning the mountain down with his big toe.

BANA
[BHAGAVATA PURANA]

When Shiva retreated into meditation, he would be gone for years at a time. Parvati would be alone at home and she was often tearful, longing for a companion. Bana, the king of the barbarians, saw an opportunity to please Shiva and sent his daughter Usha as a companion for Parvati.

Sure enough, Shiva was greatly pleased and he gifted a thousand arms to Bana as his reward. Bana crowed in delight and used his arms to terrorise the earth. The gods watched all this in dismay. Unable to withstand the suffering they witnessed, they approached Vishnu and begged his help in vanquishing Bana.

Vishnu came down to earth, incarnated as Krishna. Usha, Bana's young daughter, was smitten by Krishna's grandson, Aniruddha. Bana was enraged when he discovered this, however, and he imprisoned Aniruddha. That was the moment Krishna was waiting for—he attacked Bana's kingdom and a fierce battle was fought, in which Bana was killed.

Krishna liberated his grandson and the marriage of Aniruddha and Usha was celebrated with great pomp and festivity. They were made King and Queen of Bana's kingdom and together, they established the rule of dharma.

While Shiva represents that aspect of God which is closer to nature, transcending social codes and cultural constructions, Vishnu represents that aspect of God which is closer to culture, instituting and maintaining dharma, the code of righteous conduct. His laws determine what is appropriate and what is not, in nature and in society. Unlike Shiva, therefore, Vishnu has standards and values. He participates in worldly affairs with what some may consider greater responsibility. This is best expressed in their individual forms. While Shiva appears as a hermit who makes no attempt to be part of society, Vishnu appears as a warrior-king who is very much part of society.

Difference between Shiva and Vishnu

	Shiva (Hara)	Vishnu (Hari)
Abode	Snow-capped mountain	Ocean of milk
Clothes	Animal skins	Silk robes
Cosmetic	Ash	Sandal Paste
Jewellery	Snakes and Beads	Flowers and Gold
Association with the creative aspect of God, Brahma	Carries Brahma's skull as his begging bowl	The lotus that rises from his navel gives birth to Brahma
Offering	Raw milk	Butter

When Hinduism became less ritualistic and more theistic, and old Vedic gods such as Indra and Agni waned in significance, two schools emerged, based on the deity chosen to represent God. For Shaivas, the ascetic Shiva was the absolute manifestation of God. For Vaishnavas, the worldly Vishnu was the absolute manifestation of God. The rivalry between the two schools was great. Vaishavas refused to eat with, or marry, Shaivas. The Vaishnavas identified themselves with a caste mark that was painted vertically on the forehead. Shaivas identified themselves with a caste mark that was painted horizontally. In narratives, many attempts were made to show Shiva as being greater than Vishnu.

SHARABHA
[SHIVA PURANA]

The demon Hiranyakasipu was invincible. He had obtained a boon from Brahma that made him extremely powerful. After practising severe austerities to please Brahma, he had been granted his wish by the Creator—he would die only at the hands of a creature that was neither man nor beast. Aware that such a creature was not to be found on earth, Hiranyakasipu unleashed a reign of terror.

Vishnu appeared on earth in the form of Narasimha, a creature that was part man, part lion, in order to vanquish Hiranyakasipu. But after killing the demon, Vishnu refused to abandon the terrible avatar. He was as if possessed by the demon he had killed and his fury spread mayhem in the world.

Narasimha had to be stopped somehow and the gods pleaded with Shiva for intervention. Shiva took the form of Sharabha, a monster that was part animal, part bird, with eight feet and enormous claws. Sharabha took to the skies with a mighty roar that shook the earth. Grabbing Narasimha in his powerful talons, Sharabha subdued him.

Shiva thus forced Vishnu to shed an incarnation that had outlived its purpose.

Vaishnavas, in their scriptures, were equally determined to position Vishnu as being greater than Shiva. The rivalry between them became fierce and intense. Even today major Vaishnava shrines like Tirupati do not have an image of Shiva or his children. Even Ganesha is not acknowledged at the start of a ceremony. Instead, Vishnu's herald, Vishwaksena, is invoked.

In South India, the rivalry between sects worshipping Shiva and sects worshipping Vishnu reached such heights in medieval times that stories came into being to demonstrate the superiority of Shiva over Vishnu and vice versa. It is said that Shiva took the form of a monster called Sharabha to tame Narasimha, the most violent and monstrous form of Vishnu.

THE ASH DEMON
[VISHNU PURANA]

An asura harboured great ambition in his evil heart. He sought to be all-powerful but he knew he would need special powers. He performed severe penance and invoked Shiva.

"You have pleased me with your devotion," said Shiva. "Ask what you will and it shall be granted." That was what the asura was longing to hear. "If I so much as place my hand on the head of another, may he be reduced to a heap of ashes, my Lord," he asked. Bound by his promise, Shiva said, "So be it."

The wily asura was keen to test his new-found power and he decided to try it out on Shiva himself! Shiva realised his intentions too late and had to run for his life, with the demon in hot pursuit. Vishnu watched in dismay and knew Shiva was in grave danger. He decided to intervene and took the form of the alluring enchantress, Mohini.

Mohini waylaid the asura as he chased Shiva. Her beautiful smile and shapely form enticed him. Overwhelmed with desire, he begged the nymph to marry him. "Not unless you dance like me," she said coyly and the asura agreed willingly. Mohini began to sway and dance, with the asura following her movements. He copied every move she made, every expression, even the movement of her eyes.

At one point in the dance, in a graceful move, Mohini placed her palm upon her own head and the asura, blinded by desire, followed suit. Instantly, he was reduced to ashes. And Vishnu, in the form of Mohini, had rescued Lord Shiva from the ash-demon.

In the following narrative, Shiva is such a simpleton that he cannot distinguish between man and woman. This earns Shiva the title of Bhole-nath, the guileless god. Rather than make Shiva seem weak, this quality makes him more endearing to his devotees. They realise that Shiva is so evolved that the difference between man and woman is of no consequence to him. He recognises differences imposed by society on gender as being ephemeral and often artificial. His attention is on the sexless, gender-less soul rather than on the biology that envelops it. This leads to encounters that make Shiva sexually ambiguous to the onlooker. Reading homo-eroticism into the narratives —either positively or negatively—depends on the perception of the onlooker, born of prejudices that are based on social standards. Shiva projects nothing. His mind is clear of any and all social standards.

Mohini is the enchantress form of Vishnu. With this form, he seduced the asuras and ensured that the elixir of immortality was consumed only by the devas. *Illustration by author.*

EMBRACING MOHINI
[SABARIMALAI STHALA PURANA]

Vishnu had taken on the form of Mohini, the enchantress. So alluring was her form, so graceful her every move, that even Shiva was seduced. He embraced her and spilt his semen. From their union was born a son, Manikantha.

Mohini gave the baby Manikantha to the childless Chera king, who was delighted to have a son to rule after him. Manikantha was raised a prince. He was a talented boy and became a gifted warrior. But he had also inherited the ascetic character of Shiva.

A few years after he had been adopted, his foster mother bore the king a son. Now she no longer wanted Manikantha to succeed the king to the throne. Eager to secure power for her own son, she feigned a severe illness. She was in terrible pain, she cried, and did not have long to live. The only thing that could save her life was the milk of a tigress, she said.

Manikantha offered to get her the milk of a tigress and at once set off on his quest. He had to travel far and through dense forests where he was attacked by many demons. Undaunted, he overpowered them all and returned to the palace with the milk of a tigress for his mother.

In order to make sure that she was completely cured, he happily gave up his right to the throne. In keeping with his character, he became an ascetic and spent the rest of his life on the top of a hill that overlooked his father's kingdom.

Vishnu takes the form of Mohini or the celestial enchantress in his capacity as protector of the world. He needs heroes to rid the earth of trouble-making demons. By taking advantage of Shiva's innocence, by stirring the unfettered desire of his loins, Vishnu makes the fire-churning ascetic shed his semen out of which are born warrior-gods such as Manikantha.

Manikantha or Ayyappa represents the reconciliation between sects worshipping Shiva and Vishnu. He is the son of Shiva and Mohini. Like Shiva, he is an ascetic. Like Vishnu, he protects the world of his devotees. *Poster art.*

In the Shiva Purana, Hanuman is the son created when Shiva and Mohini unite. Hanuman is the monkey-god in Hindu mythology, associated with superhuman strength, intelligence, humility, and discipline. The sons of both Shiva and Vishnu kill demons and serve as earth-guardians. Both are hyper-masculine yet celibate, avoiding female company. Hanuman is the ascetic-warrior who protects the chastity of women and gives strength to men to follow the monastic ideal. Manikantha is the ascetic-warrior who blesses men only after they display control over their senses.

Hanuman, the monkey-god, was born when Shiva spilt his semen at the sight of Mohini. This son of Shiva and Vishnu became the guardian of the Goddess and the servant of God. *North Indian miniature.*

Demons once sought to take advantage of Shiva's inability to differentiate between man and woman in order to cause a rift between Shiva and Shakti. The attempt was a failure.

DEATH OF ADI
[MATSYA PURANA]

The demon Adi was on a murderous mission. He wanted to kill Shiva. He took the form of Parvati and sought Shiva's embrace. He had come well prepared, having implanted poisonous teeth in his "vagina" that would kill Shiva with potent venom. Shiva knew that this was not his wife Parvati but that it was the demon Adi laying a trap for him. He started making love with such intense passion that Adi was not able to cope with his ardour. Shiva's virility thrust into him like a thunderbolt and soon, Adi lay dead in Shiva's arms.

Shiva is so innocent that he sees no difference between sandal paste and ash, between ox and bull, between garden and crematorium, between poison and milk. His exasperated consort also realises that her guileless consort does not appreciate the meaning of a wife and the exclusivity of her affections for her husband.

A WIFE FOR RAVANA
[FOLKLORE]

Ravana, the ten-headed demon king, was an ardent devotee of Shiva. He performed sincere tapasya to invoke Shiva. The innocent Lord was pleased by his devotion and granted him a boon.

"I want the Goddess as my wife," Ravana demanded audaciously.

"So be it," replied Shiva.

When Parvati heard of this, she was enraged. But not with Shiva. She knew her Lord was innocent and he had behaved exactly as she had expected him to. He had responded to a devotee's penance, without giving a second thought to the implications of his boon. No, it was not he who incurred Parvati's wrath—it was the vile Ravana who had taken advantage of her innocent husband.

Parvati decided to teach him a lesson. She transformed a toad into a damsel who was the very likeness of herself. She let the toad-damsel loose on Mount Kailasa. Ravana met the damsel on the slopes of the mountain and believed her to be Parvati. He whisked her away to his island kingdom, Lanka, and made her his queen. She was known as Mandodari, she-who-was-once-a-toad.

Marriage is a social construct. Fidelity is a cultural demand, not a natural urge. Though willing to participate in the world, and make love to the Goddess, Shiva stays out of social structures. When social structures collapse, then taboos like rape, infidelity, incest and homosexuality can hold no ground. Society bridles the sexual urge. Society channels the desires of men and women in ways it deems fit. But what is fit varies from society to society.

While incest may be a taboo in most societies, polygyny (one man with many wives), polyandry (one woman with many husbands), sex hospitality, or homosexuality may be accepted in one society but not in another. Rules accepted by a society in one period of history change in another. What is appropriate once may not be appropriate always.

This explains why Shiva's narratives portray him simultaneously as monastic, monogamous, polygamous, and even sexually ambiguous. He is one who is always distant from society. He is unaffected by its rules and is therefore always challenging them.

Shiva's Sexual Spectrum

Monastic	Kills Kandarpa, the god of sex, love, lust, and longing
Monogamy	Makes his consort, Shakti, who is the Goddess, the left half of his body
Polygamy	The mountain-goddess, Parvati, sits on his lap while the river-goddess, Ganga, sits on his head
Sexually Ambiguous	Spills semen at the sight of Mohini, the female form of Vishnu, a male deity

In the following narrative, Shiva is unable to appreciate a woman's horrified reaction when he blesses her with five husbands.

DRAUPADI'S HUSBAND
[SKANDA PURANA]

Draupadi once invoked Shiva and asked for a husband with five ideal qualifications:

He should be king.
He should be strong.
He should be a skilled archer.
He should be handsome.
He should be knowledgeable.

Shiva granted her wish, saying, "You will have all the five husbands that you desire."

Draupadi was horrified but Shiva's boon had been granted. He was so removed from things mundane that he failed to see any difference between a husband with five ideal qualifications, and five husbands, each with an ideal qualification! And that is how Draupadi came to be married to the five sons of Pandu.

Yudhisthira was a king.
Bhima was a mighty wrestler.
Arjuna was an archer without parallel.
Nakula was the most handsome man in the world.
Sahadeva was the most knowledgeable of all.

Shiva's mind is purified of all standards and divisions. So, on his wedding day, he feels no qualms about offering snakes, skulls, and skeletons as gifts to the mother of his bride. She faints, of course. And Shiva stands bewildered while his consort-to-be, Parvati, looks on with endearing affection at the God unused to worldly ways.

The third eye is perhaps the greatest symbol of Shiva's transcendent nature, one that is unfettered by ideas that divide beauty from ugliness, left from right, top from bottom, past from future, men from women, minerals from plants, and plants from animals. This eye has no eyebrow; it looks neither to the left nor to the right, neither to the top nor to the bottom. It has no orientation. Shiva opens his third eye and reduces Kandarpa, the god of desire, to ashes. This is because desire presupposes a division between the subject who desires and the object that is desirable. Desire also presupposes a division between objects that are undesirable and objects that are desirable. Shiva is beyond such divides. He therefore cannot succumb to the love-god's arrows. The love-god fails, and ceases to be, as Shiva has no frame of reference through which to peep into the garden of sensual delights. A creature born of this third eye possesses the characteristics of the very same eye: though born of a god, it is demonic and it cannot distinguish between a mother and a woman.

Shiva impaling Andhaka, who was born in darkness, when both Shiva's eyes were shut. Hence Andhaka did not possess the intellectual power to distinguish mother from woman. *Temple carving from Belur, Karnataka.*

KILLER OF ANDHAKA
[VAMANA PURANA]

Parvati was in a playful mood. She crept up on Shiva and closed his eyes with her palms. Instantly, the world was plunged into darkness, as Shiva's left eye was the sun and the right eye was the moon. Shiva knew that the beings on earth would not survive without light and he opened his third eye.

The third eye was extremely powerful and the heat it radiated made Parvati perspire profusely. From the beads of her perspiration, a child was born. He was called Andhaka—the one born of darkness—because he was born when Shiva's eyes were covered.

Shiva gave Andhaka to the childless demon-king Hiranyayaksha. Andhaka was raised among the demons and he eventually became their ruler. He had performed great tapasya and Brahma had granted him a boon—he would be killed only if he looked upon his own mother with lust. Andhaka was sure that would never happen, as he believed he had no mother.

Andhaka derived great power from his boon and led his armies into a fierce battle with the gods. He defeated them and became the ruler of the three worlds. His kingdom now stretched to all corners of the universe. Such a vast and powerful kingdom needed a queen, he thought. He was told there was none more fit to be queen of the universe than the beautiful Parvati.

Andhaka knew Parvati was a mountain princess who had given up the comforts of her father's palace to win over and wed Shiva, the ascetic god. Andhaka went to Shiva's abode at once and began to woo Parvati. He made extravagant pledges of love, promises of gifts and riches, but Parvati was not interested. Refusing to take no for an answer, Andhaka decided to take her away by force.

Parvati cried out to Shiva for help. Shiva was enraged when he saw Andhaka dragging his wife away. He roared in anger and impaled Andhaka with his trident. Andhaka bled till his body was reduced to a bag of bones. Shiva kept him imprisoned and impaled for eons. As he lay there, floating between life and death, he realised that he was the son of Shiva and Parvati. He begged their forgiveness and spent the rest of his life singing praises of the divine couple.

Andhaka, like Ravana, wants to make Shiva's wife his queen. In the Padma Purana, another demon-king called Jalandhara wants to kill Shiva so that he can marry Parvati. Since Shiva's consort is the Goddess who embodies the material world, the desire to marry the Goddess seems like an allegory to lord over the material world. Tapasya is the common method used to achieve this goal. Unlike Shiva, who uses tapasya to know himself and attain sat-chitta-ananda, demons use tapasya to control the world. These narratives bring out the conflict between the ascetics, who are philosophers and metaphysicians, and those who are alchemists and sorcerers. The former want samadhi, liberation from the cycle of rebirths, understanding of the true nature of things, and union with the divine. The latter want siddhi, control over the cycle of rebirths, and manipulation over the forces of nature.

In early Hinduism, both samadhi and siddhi could be achieved either by the intellectual Vedic way or the more sensual Tantrik way. As Hinduism evolved, the Vedic way became more monastic and inward looking while the Tantrik way continued its focus on the outer, alchemical realities, which included sex and violence. Eventually, the spiritual goal of samadhi was identified with the Vedic way while the latter material goal of siddhi was identified with the Tantrik way, causing

Tantra to fall into disrepute in later Hinduism. As Hinduism transformed, the Vedic way saw the material world as Maya, enchanting delusion. They craved for Vidya, liberating wisdom. Both Maya and Vidya are forms of the Goddess. The Tantrik way saw the Goddess as Shakti or power. Through her and in her, they found both, spells to control the world, and knowledge to break free from the world.

The Goddess embodies the problem that is life. She is also the medium of the solution. It is she who makes Shiva a teacher—first by provoking him into confrontation and then by questioning him about the means by which he overpowers her. After turning the hermit into a householder, the Goddess repeatedly questions her husband, forcing him to reflect on the reality that he had shut his eyes to, and to share his wisdom with the world. The conversations between God and Goddess were occasionally overheard by seers and sages and transmitted to the world in the form of scriptures now known as the Veda and the Tantra.

Uma-Maheshwara images represent marital harmony and interdependence between the soul and matter, between the divine within and the divine without. *Illustration by author.*

THE BIRTH OF MASTYENDRANATH
[NAV-NATH CHARITRA]

Shiva's consort Parvati was also known as Uma or Gauri. One day, she asked Shiva to explain the reason for the existence of the world as experienced through the senses. She begged him to enlighten her. Shiva was wary, as this was deep and profound knowledge. But he did not want to displease her either, so he agreed to enlighten her, on the condition that she would not reveal the secret to anyone.

To ensure complete privacy during the transmission of the knowledge, Shiva took her to a cave, buried deep in a valley of the Himalayas. He spoke to her at length, explaining how the world comes into being, how it transforms, and why it transforms.

Now, in that cave, there was a little pond, which was home to a tiny fish. He overheard the divine conversation and having gained the knowledge, he was able to transform himself into a man. He climbed out of the pond and walked out of the cave. He travelled the earth, sharing with everyone what he had heard Shiva tell Parvati. He was known as Matsyendranath. He had eight disciples who went to the eight corners of the world, carrying the word of Shiva.

Shiva as Dakshinamurti, the teacher of teachers, who faces south, the direction of death, hence change. With his wisdom he helps man cope with the vagaries of life. He sits under the Banyan tree and places his right foot on the ground. Both the Banyan tree and the right side of the body are associated with stillness and the unchanging reality of the soul. *Illustration by author.*

On the southern wall of many temples in South India one finds Shiva sitting under a Banyan tree, giving a discourse to ascetics; his right foot crushes a demon while his left foot rests folded on his lap. This form of Shiva is called Dakshinamurti—the teacher who faces the southern direction.

In East India, the Goddess is popularly worshipped as Dakshina-kali —the wanton goddess who approaches from the south. The Goddess is visualised as a naked, dark woman with unbound hair, drinking blood, brandishing a sickle, and bedecked with human heads. Shiva Dakshinamurti thus sits facing the approaching Goddess. In narratives, he stops her march.

According to Hindu geomancy or Vastu-shastra, the south is the realm of Yama, god of death. North is the realm of Kubera, god of abundance. South is thus associated with the passing away of things while north with the permanence of things. Hence, the Goddess, who embodies the temporal world of senses, comes from the south simultaneously projecting ideas of creation (naked and erotic) and ideas of destruction (bloodthirsty and violent). Looking upon her creates anxiety and excitement—anxiety, because in a changing world nothing is certain; excitement, because her naked body holds the promise of pleasure and rebirth.

Shiva, on the other hand, looks calm, composed, and serene, as he imparts wisdom from the north under the Banyan tree, which is renowned for its longevity (permanence), and its shade (wisdom). Most people deny, repress, and turn their backs on Kali. Shiva, however, confronts and subdues Kali.

Shiva with an upraised leg is known as Urdhva Nataraja who takes the stance to embarass the Goddess into submission. *Illustration by author.*

THE UPRAISED LEG
[TAMIL TEMPLE LORE]

Kali had been created to destroy the demons. And she revelled in her role, killing them all and drinking their blood. But having finished her task, she did not stop. She continued killing and destroying everything in her path. The gods were terrified at the wanton destruction but even they were powerless to stop her. Along with Brahma and Vishnu, they approached Shiva and sought his help.

Shiva agreed to stop her. He blocked her path as she roamed the world in a wild frenzy, and challenged her to a dance competition. "If you can defeat me in dance, you can behead me and drink my blood too," he told the wild goddess. Kali bit the bait. She channelled all her energy and fury away from destruction and into dance. The gods watched Shiva and Kali dance with bated breath. The earth trembled with the passionate stamping of their feet. The sun and the moon ducked for cover behind the hills as the divine couple moved their arms and legs to a frenzied beat.

Shiva and Kali danced for eons. Their skills were well matched. Kali could do what Shiva could. Shiva could replicate each of Kali's moves. Neither was able to outshine the other. Then suddenly, Shiva raised his left leg so that his left knee was behind his left ear and his left foot was over his head. Kali began to follow him but was stopped by her innate feminine modesty. She could not attain that stance without exposing her private parts to the whole world. Smiling shyly, she conceded defeat. The gods applauded Shiva's ingenuity, as Kali was now transformed into a modest maiden. Shiva became known now as the Lord of Dance, Nataraja. The

pose he had struck was called the Urdhva
Nataraja, the posture that tamed a wild goddess.

By overpowering Kali, Shiva empowers those who feel overwhelmed by the sheer power of nature. From indifferent ascetic, he transforms into the informed teacher whose wisdom enables one to fearlessly face the reality of material life.

Water is the most common Hindu symbol of the material world. Life is fluid, ever changing, never still, like water. It takes the shape of the container. But the essence of water does not change. If water is the world, then the vessel is the mind. Vessels can change shape; they can break; but the water continues to flow.

When the world was in its infancy, when there were no "things" in the world, matter existed as a formless and nameless mass poetically described as the "ocean of milk". The world seemed bleak, meaningless, and purposeless. It lacked joy. There were no stimuli to delight the senses.

The father-god, Prajapati, had two sets of sons, Adityas and Daityas, born of two wives, Aditi and Diti. They set about churning the ocean determined to create things with name and form that would transform the cosmos into a container of myriad experiences. But they did not bargain for what emerged from the ocean.

With the joys came the sorrows; with the nectar came venom. Fearing that the sorrow and venom would destroy the world, they turned to the supreme ascetic-teacher, Shiva. He was indifferent to what was desirable and what was not. He was beyond positive and negative. Only he could accept what no one else could. Only he could deliver them and ensure that the world was not overwhelmed by misery.

THE BLUE THROAT
[SHIVA PURANA]

Once Lakshmi, the goddess of wealth and fortune, disappeared from the three worlds. She jumped into the ocean of milk and dissolved into it completely. But both, the gods and the demons, wanted her back at any cost. They decided to churn the ocean with Mount Mandara as the spindle. They wound Vasuki, the serpent, around Mandara, to serve as the churning rope. In order to provide Mandara with a stable base, they used the king of turtles, Akupara. He would keep Mandara afloat on his back.

The demons then grasped Vasuki by the tail end, while the gods grasped the neck. They pulled and tugged, providing force and counter-force for the churning action. They churned the ocean of milk for eons. Eventually their efforts were rewarded and Lakshmi emerged from the ocean, along with many wonderful things that included Amrita, the nectar of immortality.

The gods and demons were delighted at having retrieved Lakshmi from the ocean. They were examining the other fruits of their labour, when suddenly the ocean spewed out the deadly venom, Halahal. There was panic among both sides. They were desperate to possess everything that they had churned out of the ocean but neither side wanted the venom. In fact, they wanted to get rid of it as fast as possible. In their desperation, they cried out to Shiva for help.

Shiva, the ascetic, made no distinction between poisons and elixirs. He took Halahal and raised it to his lips. The Goddess saw her Lord swallowing the poison and feared its effects. She ran towards him, pressed his neck, and tied a serpent around it tightly. The poison remained in his throat and could not enter Shiva's body. That is how he came to be known as Neelkantha, the One with the Blue Throat.

Shiva drinking the poison, Halahal, at the behest of the gods. *Ilustration by author.*

In order to enjoy the pleasures of life, one must have the ability to endure or overcome the pains of life. Neither the Adityas nor the Daityas know how. Only Shiva does. He has the power to swallow Halahal. The Goddess, however, prevents the poison from leaving his neck. For if it enters his stomach, he will destroy it with his inner fire. And if pain is destroyed, then pleasure has no meaning. And without the experience of pain and pleasure, life has no meaning.

Shiva could drink the poison only because he is Yogeshwara, the lord of yoga. Yoga frees the mind and makes it pliant enough to experience life without being overwhelmed by it.

Symbols of Permanence and Impermanence

Permanence	Impermanence
Banyan Tree	Grass
Mountain	River, Ocean
Turtle	Serpent
Ash	Water

Left to himself, Shiva would have destroyed Halahal completely. And in doing so, destroyed the experience of life. The Goddess does not let him do that. The Goddess is both Kali and Gauri, the dark and the fair one. She embodies both Halahal and Amrita. One form makes no sense without the other. To destroy one means to destroy the other. The purpose of life is to experience and accept both forms of the Goddess and to discover the God who enables one to do so. Thus, the paradoxical nature of the divine without stirs one to discover the divine within.

The material world of Shakti is terrifying, because it is impermanent. Yet, in its impermanence lies the promise of renewal. In samsara, even death is impermanent. All things are reborn. One may not be able to step into the same river twice, the waters may slip between clenched fists, but rivers are life-giving. They sustain civilisations on their banks. This is affirmed by the Hindu practice of throwing the ashes of the dead into a river to ensure their rebirth. A Banyan tree may offer shade and hold the promise of permanence, but it does not let even a blade of grass grow around it, nor does it provide life-sustaining fruit. Thus the material world is characterised by opposite values. The river is impermanent and constantly flowing, yet it sustains life. The Banyan offers shade, but does not permit any life to flourish around it. In the following narrative, Shiva reconciles the two sides of the river of existence.

146

Shiva uses his matted hair to break the fall of the Ganga. She is the river of life that can sweep away the mind. His matted hair represents a mind controlled by yoga hence able to withstand the power of the river-goddess. *Poster art.*

Shiva, who once withdrew the heat of the world into himself, becomes the fountainhead of the river of life after the Goddess becomes his wife. *Illustration by author.*

DESCENT OF GANGA
[RAMAYANA]

Bhagirath's granduncles had once mistakenly accused an ascetic of theft. In a terrible rage at the insult, the ascetic had used the powers gained from continence to burn them alive. Unfortunately for the men, however, they had died before their time. As a result, Bhagirath's granduncles were not granted entry into the land of the dead and they lingered unhappily between the world of the living and the world of the dead.

They begged Bhagirath to find a way of restoring them into the cycle of rebirths. This was possible only if their ashes were cast into a river known as the Ganga. The Ganga was a mighty river that flowed in the celestial realms, as the Milky Way, and Bhagirath had no way of taking their ashes to the plane that was the abode of the gods. But he was moved by the plight of his granduncles and he decided to make the river flow on earth.

He performed such severe austerities that the gods were compelled to let the Ganga come down from the heavens and flow on earth. But the river nymph who embodied the Ganga scoffed at the idea, for she knew the power of the Ganga's flow was so strong that it could wash away the entire earth. Bhagirath thus decided to seek Shiva's help. Shiva stood atop Mount Kailasa, his arms akimbo, ready to catch the Ganga in his matted locks before she touched the ground. The Ganga leapt from the heavens in all her glory, ready to flow on the earth, but no sooner did she come in contact with Shiva's head than she found herself trapped in his mighty locks, unable to break free. She writhed in agony like a caged bird and was only allowed to leave when she agreed to a gentler flow. As the Ganga gurgled her way out of Shiva's locks through the mountains and across the plains towards the sea, she brought life and laughter on her banks. Bhagirath immersed the ashes of his ancestors in the Ganga. As foretold, his granduncles were allowed into the land of the dead, ready to be reborn.

Shiva uses his hair to tame the river of life. According to Tantra, physical strength comes from mental strength, and mental strength comes from sexual continence. Shiva, who withholds his seed for eons, has so much strength in his hair that it can contain water or restrain a river.

The Ganga embodies the world perceived by the senses; but Shiva is not swept away by the force of the Ganga's swirling waters, the symbols of material transformations. He withstands it all with ease and ends up controlling the flow. Shiva's thick matted locks are indicators of his mental strength. Through meditation and yoga, Shiva has the mental strength to withstand the force of the river of life and transform it into a nurturing force. Had the Goddess not been in his life, Shiva would have destroyed the Ganga. But with the Goddess by his side, he is sensitive to the value of the material world. Rather than burning the river-nymph as he did the love-god, he makes her his second wife. In other words, he does not withdraw the mind from all things material; he merely controls his response to its transformation.

By catching the Ganga, Shiva makes her flow gently, sustaining life along her riverbanks. Thus the energy withdrawn by tapasya is released through the binding of the Ganga. The Ganga's threat to destroy the world forces Shiva to use his bottled up tapa for the good of the world. Tapa thus transforms into the life sap, rasa, and sustains the world. In temples, a pot dripping water continuously from a hole in its base is placed atop the Shiva-linga. It represents the Ganga, the water of samsara that forces Shiva to release his tapa for the benefit and welfare of the world.

The most common ritual in Shiva temples is the pouring of water over Shiva's linga so that his energy moves outwards rather than moving inwards and benefits everyone around.

For those who still do not want anything to do with the material world, Shiva continues to serve as deliverer. In the following narrative, the devotee wants liberation from samsara. The technique used is not tapasya, but bhakti or devotion. The devotee is doomed to face death and change, yet, through Shiva, he finds absolute liberation from the merry-go-round we call life.

RESCUE OF MARKANDEYA
[SHIVA PURANA]

Markandeya's parents had been childless for a long time. Distraught at the thought of having no heir, they prayed to Shiva. Shiva had mercy on them and granted them a wish—they could have one stupid son, who would be blessed with a long life, or they could have an extremely intelligent child, who would be short-lived. After much soul-searching, they chose the latter.

Thus Markandeya was born of a boon from the great Lord, but was destined to die at sixteen. On the eve of his sixteenth birthday, Markandeya decided to spend his last remaining hours in the land of the living by praying to Lord Shiva. Yama, the god of death, appeared at the appointed hour. But Markandeya asked him to wait, as he had not yet finished his prayers. Yama laughed at the boy's ignorance. "Death waits for no man!" he shouted, and threw his noose around Markandeya's neck. As Markandeya felt his life's breath being forced out of him, he surrendered to Shiva with a final cry.

Shiva heard the boy cry out and appeared at his side. He kicked Yama aside and took Markandeya to Mount Kailasa where he lived forever as a young boy.

Shiva's abode, Kailasa or Shiva-loka, the highest heaven for Shiva's devotees, is higher than Indra's heaven where all material wants are absolutely fulfilled, and higher than Vishnu's heaven where one is free of all material wants. It is the place that one reaches by devotion. And through devotion we are able to unravel the knots in the consciousness that delude us and keep us from comprehending the true nature of things. By staying in samsara, through devotion to Shiva, by accepting every moment of life—good or bad—as the gift of Shiva, one can still attain sat-chitta-ananda, the goal of tapasya , and find that which eluded every yagna: shanti-shanti-shanti.

Shiva rescuing Markandeya from certain death. By overpowering Yama, the god of death, Shiva becomes Yamantaka, God who liberates souls from the cycle of birth and death. *Mysore art, 20th century. Image courtesy: R. G. Singh, Mysore.*

153

CONCLUSION: DECONSTRUCTING DESTRUCTION

Shiva is the divine within us—the observer of life. Shakti is the divine around us—the observation that is life. Without either there is neither. Hindu seers have expressed this mutual dependence through the symbol of the linga. Just as the linga cannot be distinguished from other cylindrical shafts without the yoni-like basin, just as the front of the linga can only be identified by the leftward orientation of the yoni's snout, one cannot understand or define oneself without understanding and defining one's world.

In the linga, the phallus does not point downward as in the missionary position of copulation. This is because Shakti is visualised as being on top of Shiva, facing north, while he lies on his back facing south. This position is known in Tantra as viparita-rati, reverse copulation. The water-basin of the linga represents the entrance of Shakti's womb—which is the world we inhabit—into which Shiva's phallus, hence his energy, is being drawn. Shiva is the inward-looking inert consciousness, whom Shakti stirs and excites so that life can happen. Shakti comes from the south, the direction associated with death and change. Shiva's wisdom gives him the power to look towards her with absolute serenity. Shakti wants Shiva to be Shankara. She wants him to acknowledge and know her, and through her, know himself.

Shiva knows Shakti to be that river of endless transformations and stimulations that can sweep away all peace of mind. Initially, for the sake of tranquility, Shiva turned away from her, withdrawing all his attention into himself like a turtle in its shell. The resulting self-containment resulted in indifference to outer reality. The physical form became unappealing to the eye (ash-smeared body). The surroundings became inhospitable to life (snow-clad mountains). Distant from the tribulations of the world, Shiva regressed into blissful inertia, a state expressed in art as an erect penis. This was not a reaction to sensory arousal; it was not intent on shedding seed, but was svayambhu or self-stirred.

By refusing to "observe" and react to the external world, Shiva invalidated the need for external reality. In doing so he threatened his own existence for there cannot be an observer without an observation. Shiva's concentrated tapa transformed him into fire whose all-devouring flames needed to be contained. Hence, the water-pot above the linga and the water-basin below. These are symbols of the Goddess who redirects Shiva's attention outwards, transforming the destructive heat into creative energy with her waters for the benefit of all. Devotees join Shakti in this beneficial transformation by reverentially pouring water on the linga during worship and collecting the water that flows down the yoni's snout. They want Shiva to become the beneveolent, boon-giving Shankara.

The endless copulation of Shakti and Shiva represents the eternal struggle between our inner and outer worlds—our desire to be Shiva and withdraw from it or our desire to be Shankara and embrace it. There is "shanti, shanti, shanti"—peace with oneself, one's world, and everything around—when the rhythm is perfect, when neither dominates the other. The purpose of yoga—whether it is hatha-yoga of the ascetic, gyana-yoga of the philosopher, bhakti-yoga of the devotee, or karma-yoga of the householder—is to unbind the consciousness and establish harmony with the material world so that we experience the eternal principle of being, sanatana dharma:

The divine inside you is God
The divine around you is Goddess
Without either there is neither
In their discovery lies wisdom
In their harmonious union lies eternal bliss

SELECT BIBLIOGRAPHY

- Bhattacharji, Sukumari. The Indian Theogony. New Delhi: Penguin Books, 2000.
- Coupe, Lawrence. Myth. London: Routledge, 1997.
- Dange, Sadashiv Ambadas. Encyclopaedia of Puranic Beliefs and Practices, Vol. 1- 5. New Delhi: Navrang, 1990.
- Danielou, Alain. Gods of Love and Ecstasy: The Traditions of Shiva and Dionysus. Rochester, Vt.: Inner Traditions International, 1992.
- ———. Hindu Polytheism. Rochester, Vt.: Inner Traditions International, 1991.
- Flood, Gavin. An Introduction to Hinduism. New Delhi: Cambridge University Press, 1998.
- Frawley, David. From the River of Heaven. Delhi: Motilal Banarsidass, 1992.
- Hawley, J. S. and D.M. Wulff, eds.. The Divine Consort. Boston: Beacon Press, 1982.
- Highwater, Jamake. Myth and Sexuality. New York: Meridian, 1990.
- Jakimowicz-Shah, Marta. Metamorphosis of Indian Gods. Calcutta: Seagull Books, 1988.
- Jayakar, Pupul. The Earth Mother. Delhi: Penguin Books, 1989.
- Kinsley, David. Hindu Goddesses. Delhi: Motilal Banarsidass, 1987.
- Klostermaier, Klaus K. Hinduism: A Short History. Oxford: Oneworld Publications, 2000.
- Knappert, Jan. An Encyclopedia of Myth and Legend: Indian Mythology. New Delhi: HarperCollins, 1992.
- Kramrisch, Stella. The Presence of Shiva. New Delhi: Motilal Banarsidass, 1988.
- Mani, Vettam. Puranic Encyclopaedia. Delhi: Motilal Banarsidass, 1996.

- Meyer, Johann Jakob. Sexual Life in Ancient India. Delhi: Motilal Banarsidass, 1989.
- O'Flaherty, Wendy Doniger, trans. Hindu Myths. Delhi: Penguin Books, 1975.
- ———. Origins of Evil in Hindu Mythology. New Delhi: Motilal Banarsidass, 1988.
- ———. The Rig Veda: An Anthology. New Delhi: Penguin Books, 1994.
- O'Flaherty, Wendy Doniger. Sexual Metaphors and Animal Symbols in Indian Mythology. New Delhi: Motilal Banarsidass, 1981.
- ———. Œiva: The Erotic Ascetic. London: Oxford University Press Paperbacks, 1981.
- Pattanaik, Devdutt. Devi: An Introduction. Mumbai: Vakil, Feffer and Simons, 2000.
- ———. Goddess in India: Five Faces of the Eternal Feminine. Rochester, Vt.: Inner Traditions International, 2000.
- ———. Hanuman: An Introduction. Mumbai: Vakil, Feffer and Simons, 2001.
- Pattanaik, Devdutt. Man Who Was a Woman and Other Queer Tales from Hindu Lore. New York: Harrington Park Press, 2001.
- ———. Shiva: An Introduction. Mumbai: Vakil, Feffer and Simons, 1997.
- ———. Vishnu: An Introduction. Mumbai: Vakil, Feffer and Simons, 1999.
- Walker, Benjamin. Hindu World, Vol 1 and 2. Delhi: Munshiram Manoharlal, 1983.
- Wilkins, W. J. Hindu Mythology. Delhi: Rupa, 1997.
- Zimmer, Heinrich. Myths and Symbols in Indian Art and Civilization. Delhi: Motilal Banarsidass, 1990.

ABOUT INDUS SOURCE

Indus Source was founded in 2003 with the objective of celebrating the diverse traditions of the world and recreating the wealth of spiritual teachings, culture, and history in a contemporary format. To this end, Indus Source is engaged in publishing books for adult as well as young readership. As a niche publishing house, all our books are created with personal interest and attention to detail. Indus Source aims to promote understanding of the Self as well as understanding between faiths and cultures, and to provide positive, spiritual insights for harmony and better living.

Visit our website www.indussource.com for more details.

Indus Source Books
PO Box 6194
Malabar Hill PO
Mumbai 400006
India
www.indussource.com
info@indussource.com